First Step in Grammar

2

Clue & Key

How to Use This Book

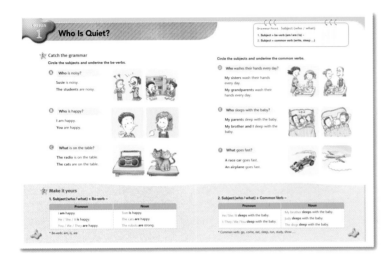

Grammar point

presents a brief summary of what the students will learn in each lesson.

Catch the grammar

presents tasks such as quizzes, readings, matching, and puzzles through which students can recognize the repetitive grammar patterns from the task.

Make it yours

provides opportunities to confirm grammar rules by organizing the patterns in the section on a grammar chart.

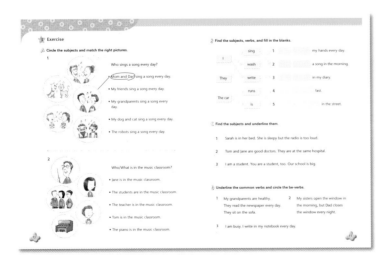

Exercise

presents various questions that students can use to check their understanding of grammar rules. Through these questions, students will have a chance to apply their understanding of the practical uses of grammar.

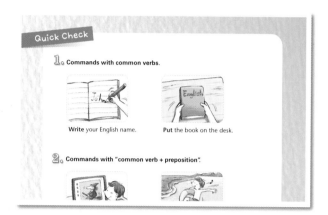

Quick Check

contains warm-up activities used as a preview and sometimes as a review to connect previous lessons with the current one.

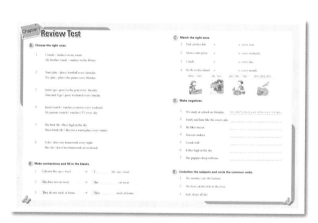

Review Test

presents cumulative questions about what the entire chapter has covered.

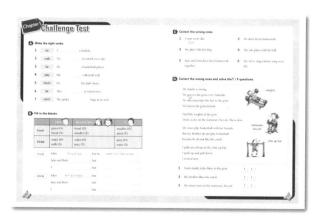

Challenge Test

presents an advanced level of questions that involve more integrated analysis so that students can deepen their understanding of grammar rules in more challenging ways.

Contents

Chapter 1

1. Commands with common verbs.

Write your English name.

Put the book on the desk.

2. Commands with "common verb + preposition".

Look at the computer.

Go to the beach.

Sit on the chair.

Listen to the radio.

Choose the right ones.

1. Sit (the chair / on the chair).

2. Open (to the window / the window).

Who Is Quiet?

⭐ Catch the grammar

Circle the subjects and underline the be-verbs.

A **Who** is noisy?

(Susie) is noisy.
(The students) are noisy.

B **Who** is happy?

I am happy.
You are happy.

C **What** is on the table?

The radio is on the table.
The cats are on the table.

⭐ Make it yours

1. Subject (who / what) + Be-verb ~

Pronoun	Noun
I **am** happy.	Tom **is** happy.
He/She/It **is** happy.	The cats **are** happy.
You/We/They **are** happy.	The robots **are** strong.

* Be-verb: am, is, are

Grammar Point **Subject (who / what)**

1. **Subject + be-verb (am / are / is) ~**
2. **Subject + common verb (write, sleep ...)**

Circle the subjects and underline the common verbs.

D **Who** washes their hands every day?

My sisters wash their hands every day.

My grandparents wash their hands every day.

E **Who** sleeps with the baby?

My parents sleep with the baby.

My brother and I sleep with the baby.

F **What** goes fast?

A race car goes fast.

An airplane goes fast.

2. Subject (who / what) + Common Verb ~

Pronoun	Noun
He / She / It **sleeps** with the baby. I / They / We / You **sleep** with the baby.	My brother **sleeps** with the baby. Judy **sleeps** with the baby. The dogs **sleep** with the baby.

* Common verb: go, come, eat, sleep, run, study, show ...

Exercise

 Circle the subjects and match the right pictures.

1

Who sings a song every day?

• (Mom and Dad) sing a song every day.

• My friends sing a song every day.

• My grandparents sing a song every day.

• My dog and cat sing a song every day.

• The robots sing a song every day.

- -

2

Who/What is in the music classroom?

• Jane is in the music classroom.

• The students are in the music classroom.

• The teacher is in the music classroom.

• Tom is in the music classroom.

• The piano is in the music classroom.

B Find the subjects, verbs, and fill in the blanks.

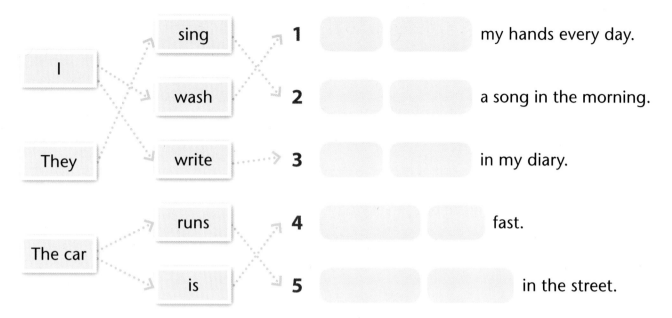

	sing	**1** _____ _____ my hands every day.
I	wash	**2** _____ _____ a song in the morning.
They	write	**3** _____ _____ in my diary.
	runs	**4** _____ _____ fast.
The car	is	**5** _____ _____ in the street.

C Find the subjects and underline them.

1   Sarah is in her bed. She is sleepy but the radio is too loud.

2   Tom and Jane are good doctors. They are at the same hospital.

3   I am a student. You are a student, too. Our school is big.

D Underline the common verbs and circle the be-verbs.

1   My grandparents are healthy.
         They read the newspaper every day.
         They sit on the sofa.

2   My sisters open the window in
         the morning, but Dad closes
         the window every night.

3   I am busy. I write in my notebook every day.

We Run Every Day.

⭐ Catch the grammar

Look and speak.

A Hi! I am Tom.

I am a singer.

I **sing** in music class every day.

I **dance** for my parents at night.

B Hi, Jane! You are a good student!

You are smart!

You **read** a book every day.

You **write** a book report every day, too.

C Hey! We are runners.

We are fast.

We **run** together.

We **jump** rope together.

⭐ Make it yours

Subject	Common Verb
I	read a newspaper every morning.
You	write an email every day.
We	run far every night.
They	jump high every night.

* Be-verb

Subject + Be-verb	
I	am a friend.
You	are a friend.
We / They	are friends.

D My sister's name is Cindy.

She is pretty.

She **sings** well. She **dances** well, too.

Verb Change   I: sing — She: _____

E My brother's name is David.

He is 5 years old.

He **reads** a picture book every night.

He **writes** his name every day.

Verb Change   You: read — He: _____

F This is my puppy.

It is black and cute.

It **runs** fast. It **jumps** well.

Verb Change   We: run — It: _____

Subject	Common Verb + -s
He She It	reads a newspaper every day.
	writes an email every day.
	runs far every morning.
	jumps high every night.

* Be-verb

Subject + Be-verb	
He	is a friend.
She	is a friend.
It	is a rat.

13

Exercise

A Choose the right ones.

1

I (am / run) in the morning.

2

He (is / likes) cookies.

3

She (is / sleeps) at 9:00.

4

They (are / ride) their bikes every day.

B Choose the right ones.

1 I am a student.

I (walk / walks) to school in the morning.

2 He is a good writer.

He (write / writes) in his diary every day.

3 They are a family.

They (love / loves) each other.

4 She is a singer.

She (sing / sings) a song every day.

5 You are a good cook.

You (cook / cooks) every day.

6 It is a fish.

It (lives / live) in the river.

7 We are good basketball players.

We (play / plays) basketball well.

Fill in the blanks.

I have many good friends in my class.

1 Kevin _____ my good friend. (**be**)

He _____ a good swimmer. (**be**)

He _____ in the pool after school. (**swim**)

We _____ together in the pool. (**swim**)

---

2 Emma _____ a good painter. (**be**)

I _____ a good painter, too. (**be**)

She _____ pictures every day. (**draw**)

I _____ pictures every day, too. (**draw**)

---

3 Jeff _____ a good helper. (**be**)

He _____ many students with their homework. (**help**)

I _____ Jeff every day. (**help**)

---

4 Jason _____ a fast runner. (**be**)

He _____ every Saturday. (**run**)

My brothers and I _____ every Saturday, too. (**run**)

---

5 Judy _____ a good writer. (**be**)

She _____ many letters to her friends. (**write**)

My sisters _____ many letters every night, too. (**write**)

She Eats Breakfast at 7:00.

 Catch the grammar

Look and speak.

A **My daily schedule**

I (You, We, They)	get up		at 6:00 every morning.
	brush	my teeth	in the bathroom.
	eat	breakfast	at 7:00.
	go	to school	at 8:00.
	study		at school.
	watch	TV	at 4:00.
	do	homework	at 7:30.
	go	to bed	at 9:00.

B **Other schedules**

The students **go** to the library <u>every month</u>.   Jan., Feb., Mar., ~ Dec.

Tim and Jason **play** football <u>every year</u>.   2011, 2012, 2013...

 Make it yours

1. Common Verb + -s

Subject	Common Verb
I / You / We / They	read, write, drink ...
He / She / It	reads, writes, drinks ...
He and she (plural)	read, write, drink ...
Students (plural)	read, write, drink ...

C **Jenny's daily schedule**

	gets up		at 6:30 every morning.
	brushes	her teeth	in the bathroom.
Jenny	eats	breakfast	at 7:00.
(He,	goes	to school	at 8:00.
She,	studies		at school.
It)	watches	TV	at 3:30.
	does	homework	at 9:00.
	goes	to bed	at 11:00.

D **Jenny's other schedule**

She **goes** to the library <u>every weekend</u>.   Saturday, Sunday

She **plays** a computer game <u>every day</u>.   Monday ~ Sunday

2. Common Verb + -es / -ies

Subject	Common Verb				
I / You / We / They	study	wash	watch	do	go
He / She / It	studies	washes	watches	does	goes

* play – plays

⭐ Exercise

Ⓐ Choose the right ones.

1 The dogs play with the ball well. They catch / catches the ball well.

The cat catch / catches mice well.

- -

2 Tom brushes / brush his teeth every morning.

We brushes / brush Dad's shoes every morning.

- -

3 I studies / study Chinese every day.

He studies / study English every day.

- -

4 Mr. Kim and Mrs. Lee play / plays with my dog.

The dog play / plays with the ball.

- -

5 We do / does our homework in our room.

My sister do / does her homework in the library.

- -

6 She go / goes swimming early on Saturday.

We go / goes to the park every weekend.

Ⓑ Match the right ones.

1 I study every day. •   • Saturday, Sunday

2 She goes swimming every month. •   • Mon., Tue., Wed., Thu., Fri., Sat., Sun.

3 He goes hiking on weekends. •   • Jan., Feb., Mar., Apr. ... December

4 My parents love skiing. They go skiing every year. •   • 2011, 2012, 2013, 2014 ...

C **Fill in the blanks.**

1 The birds eat the worms.

The hen _____ the worms, too.

2 The baby chicks cry, "cheep! cheep!"

The dog _____, "Bark! Bark!"

3 We go to church every Sunday.

Dad _____ to the mountain every Sunday.

4 The bears catch fish in the river.

The frog _____ flies in the air.

5 The cats wash their feet with their tongues.

The kitten _____ her feet with her tongue, too.

D **Fill in the blanks.**

1 He _____ breakfast at 9:00.

2 He _____ TV at 5:00.

3 He _____ his homework at 3:00.

4 He _____ a computer game at 4:00.

5 He _____ his face at 10:00.

6 He _____ at 11:00.

9:00

10:00

11:00

3:00

5:00

4:00

Word Bank   eat   do   sleep   play   wash   watch

I Do Not Get Up Early.

 Catch the grammar

Look and speak.

A I am different from my brother and sister.

I **get up** early in the morning.

They **<u>do not</u> get up** early.

They **get up** late in the morning.

I **like** pizza.

They **<u>do not</u> like** pizza.

They **like** spaghetti.

But we **<u>don't</u> like** scary movies.

B My sister is different from my brother. They are not the same.

She **likes** ice cream.

He **<u>does not</u> like** ice cream.

He **likes** iced coffee.

She **studies** at home.

He **<u>doesn't</u> study** at home.

He **studies** at the library.

 Make it yours

1. I / You / We / They: do not (= don't) + Verb

	I / You / We / They
Affirmative	I (You / We / They) like the dog.
Negative	I (You / We / They) do not like the dog.
Contraction	I (You / We / They) don't like the dog.

* Plural subjects: The students / Tim and Judy + do not like ~

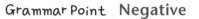

Grammar Point Negative

1. **I / You / We / They**: do not (= don't) + verb

2. **He / She / It**: does not (= doesn't) + verb

C They are animals, but they are different.

The giraffes **eat** leaves.

The lions **do not** **eat** leaves.

They **eat** meat.

The frog **lives** in the pond.

The seal **does not** **live** in the pond.

It **lives** in the sea.

The duck **swims** in the pond.

The turtle **doesn't** **swim** in the pond.

It **swims** in the sea.

2. He / She / It: does not (= doesn't) + Verb

	He / She / It
Affirmative	He(She / It) likes donuts.
Negative	He(She / It) does not like donuts.
Contraction	He(She / It) doesn't like donuts.

* Singular subjects: The student / Tim / Judy + does not like ~

3 Exercise

A Choose the right ones.

1 On a cold day, I   do not / does not   wear shorts.

2 On a hot day, we   do not / does not   wear coats.

3 This is an owl. It   do not / does not   sleep at night.

4 This is Mr. Lee. He   do not / does not   go to school on Saturday.

5 They   do not / does not   play outside on rainy days.

B Choose the right ones.

1 Jane likes baseball.

   But Jane does not (like / likes) football.

2 The airplane flies on sunny days.

   But it does not (fly / flies) on stormy days.

3 The duck plays in the water.

   But it does not (play / plays) in the mud.

4 The frogs eat flies.

   But they do not (eat / eats) ants.

C Fill in the blanks.

1 like   My grandfather _____ coffee, but he does not _____ milk.

2 play   We _____ on sunny days, but we do not _____ on rainy days.

3 sleep   She _____ late on weekends, but she does not _____ late on school days.

22

4 swim · She _____ in the swimming pool, but he does not _____ there.

5 do · He _____ homework early, but his brother does not _____ homework early.

D Fill in the blanks.

1

The bird eats worms.

But it _____ _____ eat leaves.

2

The dogs like sticks.

But they _____ _____ like worms.

3

The dolphins live in the sea.

They _____ _____ live in the pond.

4

The elephant eats peanuts.

But it _____ _____ eat meat.

E Make negatives.

1 He likes soccer.

2 I go to the gym every day.

3 You eat cookies every morning.

4 They play games every day.

5 She cooks well.

6 It flies high in the sky.

7 We ride our bikes every night.

Review Test

A Choose the right ones.

1   I (study / studies) in my room.

     My brother (study / studies) in the library.

2   Tom (play / plays) football every Saturday.

     We (play / plays) the piano every Monday.

3   Jenny (go / goes) to the gym every Tuesday.

     Tom and I (go / goes) to church every Sunday.

4   Jason (watch / watches) a movie every weekend.

     My parents (watch / watches) TV every day.

5   The bird (fly / flies) high in the sky.

     These birds (fly / flies) to a warm place every winter.

6   I (do / does) my homework every night.

     She (do / does) her homework on weekends.

B Make contractions and fill in the blanks.

1   I do not like spicy food.   →   I _____ like spicy food.

2   She does not eat meat.   →   She _____ eat meat.

3   They do not study at home.   →   They _____ study at home.

C Match the right ones.

1 Dad catches fish • • every year.

2 Mom cooks pizza • • every weekend.

3 I study • • every day.

4 We fly to the island • • every month.

| Mon. ~ Sun. | Sat., Sun. | Jan., Feb., ~ Dec. | 2011, 2012, 2013 ... |

D Make negatives.

1 We study at school on Monday.   We don't study at school on Monday.

2 Emily and Jane like the sweet cake.   _____.

3 He likes soccer.   _____.

4 You eat cookies.   _____.

5 I cook well.   _____.

6 It flies high in the sky.   _____.

7 The puppies sleep with me.   _____.

E Underline the subjects and circle the common verbs.

1 The monkey eats the banana.

2 The bear catches fish in the river.

3 Judy sleeps all day.

Challenge Test

A **Write the right verbs.**

1 be I _____ a student.

2 walk We _____ to school every day.

3 be He _____ a basketball player.

4 play She _____ volleyball well.

5 brush He _____ his dad's shoes.

6 be They _____ in school now.

7 catch The spider _____ bugs in its web.

B **Fill in the blanks.**

	John	Jane and Betty	I
Food	pizza (O) bread (X)	bread (O) noodles (X)	noodles (O) pizza (X)
Drink	water (O) milk (X)	water (O) juice (X)	juice (O) water (X)

(Food) John _____likes pizza_____, but he _____does not like bread_____.

Jane and Betty _____, but _____.

I _____, but _____.

(Drink) John _____drinks water_____, but _____.

Jane and Betty _____, but _____.

I _____, but _____.

C Correct the wrong ones.

1　I runs every day.
　　run

2　He don't do his homework.

3　She play with her dog.

4　The cats plays with the ball.

5　Jane and Tom does their homework together.

6　Mr. Terry sing a funny song every day.

D Correct the wrong ones and solve the T / F questions.

My family is strong.

We <u>goes</u> to the gym every Saturday.
　　go
We <u>does not rides</u> the bus to the gym.

We run to the gym on foot.

Dad lifts weights at the gym.

Mom cycles on the stationary bicycle. She is slow.

My sister <u>play</u> basketball with her friends.

But my brother <u>do not play</u> basketball because he <u>do not like</u> the coach.

I <u>pulls</u> myself up on the chin-up bar.

I push up and pull down.

I <u>is</u> tired now.

weights

stationary bicycle

chin-up bar

1　Tom's family rides bikes to the gym.　　T　F

2　His brother likes the coach.　　T　F

3　His mom rides on the stationary bicycle.　　T　F

Review with More - Pronoun & Verb

| Who (subject) — Singular | | Be-verb / Common Verb | |
Noun	Pronoun		
	I	am	a student.
		eat	bread every morning.
	You	are	my art teacher.
		eat	rice every morning.
Tom	He	is	my gym teacher.
		eats	donuts.
Mrs. Smith	She	is	my neighbor.
		eats	bananas.
The dog	It	is	hungry now.
		eats	bones.

Quiz

1. Tom exercises at the gym every day.

   = _____ exercises at the gym every day.

2. The dog plays on the grass.

   = _____ plays on the grass.

3. Mr. Woods _____ to the office.

   = _____ walks to the office.

4. Mrs. Smith visits us on weekends.

   = _____ visits us on weekends.

5. Jane studies Chinese at school.

   = _____ studies Chinese at school.

Who (subject) — Plural		Be-verb / Common Verb	
Noun	Pronoun		
She and I	We	are	sisters.
		eat	hamburgers every afternoon.
You and I	We	are	cousins.
		eat	chicken every day.
You and Mr. Smith	You	are	policemen.
		eat	noodles.
You and he	You	are	friends.
		eat	oranges.
Mr. Kim and Mrs. Lee	They	are	at the gym now.
		eat	cookies.
My friends	They	are	nice.
		eat	candies.

Quiz

1. The pen and the pencil are in the bag.

= _____ are in the bag.

2. She and I like the dog.

= _____ like the dog.

3. Mrs. Franks and Mr. Woods walk to the office.

= _____ walk to the office.

4. You and she are late.

= _____ are late.

5. She and he _____ many books every day.

= _____ read many books every day.

Chapter 2

1. Be-verb questions and answers: I / You / We / They

Question		Answer	
Be-verb	Subject		
Am	I ~?	Yes, you are.	No, you are not.
Are	you ~?	Yes, I am.	No, I am not.
Are	we ~?	Yes, we are.	No, we are not.
Are	they ~?	Yes, they are.	No, they are not.

2. Be-verb questions and answers: He / She / It

Question		Answer	
Be-verb	Subject		
Is	he ~?	Yes, he is.	No, he is not.
Is	she ~?	Yes, she is.	No, she is not.
Is	it ~?	Yes, it is.	No, it is not.

Answer the questions.

1. Are you Dr. Miller?

_____, _____.

2. Is he a pilot?

_____, _____.

Do You Live in an Apartment?

⭐ Catch the grammar

Read and answer the questions.

Ⓐ The worms **live** under the ground.
But the squirrels **live** in the tree.

I **live** in an apartment.
But Emily **lives** in a house.

his art class

Ⓑ I **go** to an art class every Friday.
He **goes** to an art class every Saturday.

my art class

Ⓒ I **like** computer games.
Jim **likes** card games.

⭐ Make it yours

1. Do you (I / we / they) + Common Verb ~?

Question	Do you (I / we / they) live in an apartment?		
Answer	**Yes**, I (you / we / they) do. (= Yes, I live in an apartment.)		
	No, I (you / we / they) don't. (= No, I don't live in an apartment.)		

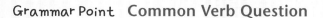

Grammar Point **Common Verb Question**

1. **Do you (I / we / they) + common verb ~?**
2. **Does he (she / it) + common verb ~?**

Do the squirrels **live** in the tree?

 Yes, they **do**. (= Yes, they **live** in the tree.)

 No, they **don't**. (= No, they don't **live** in the tree.)

Does Emily **live** in an apartment?

 Yes, she **does**. (= Yes, she **lives** in an apartment.)

 No, she **doesn't**. (= No, she doesn't **live** in an apartment.)

Do you **go** to an art class every Saturday?

 Yes, I **do**. (= Yes, I **go** to art class every Saturday.)

 No, I **don't**. (= No, I don't **go** to art class every Saturday.)

Does Jim **like** computer games?

 Yes, he **does**. (= Yes, he **likes** computer games.)

 No, he **doesn't**. (= No, he doesn't **like** computer games.)

2. Does he (she / it) + Common Verb ~?

Question	Does he (she / it) live in a house?
Answer	**Yes,** he (she / it) does. (= Yes, he lives in a house.)
	No, he (she / it) doesn't. (= No, he doesn't live in a house.)

3 Exercise

 Choose the right ones.

Question	Answer
1 (Does / Do) she study at the library?	Yes, she (does / do).
2 (Does / Do) you watch TV at night?	No, I (doesn't / don't).
3 (Does / Do) Tom like spicy food?	No, he (doesn't / don't).
4 (Does / Do) they study on Sunday?	Yes, they (does / do).
5 (Does / Do) he go to class in the morning?	Yes, he (does / do).

Choose the right ones.

1   A: Do the hamsters (run / runs) on the wheel all day?

     B: Yes, they (do / does).

2   A: Do you (ride / rides) your bike every afternoon?

     B: No, I (don't / doesn't).

3   A: Does the kitten (cry / cries) "Bark! Bark!"?

     B: No, it (don't / doesn't).

Meow!

4   A: Does he (live / lives) in a castle?

     B: No, he (don't / doesn't).

5   A: Does she (do / does) her homework every evening?

     B: Yes, she (do / does).

C Make the questions.

1 | She sleeps on the bed. |

···▸ _____ she _____ on the bed?

2 | He talks fast. |

···▸ _____ he _____ fast?

3 | Mrs. Johnson studies in the library on weekends. |

···▸ _____ Mrs. Johnson _____ in the library on weekends?

4 | They drink milk in the morning. |

···▸ _____ they _____ milk in the morning?

D Make contractions and rewrite.

1 No, I do not like the music. ⇨ _____

2 No, she does not swim every day. ⇨ _____

E Fill in the blanks.

1 A: Does he go to school at 7:00 a.m.?

 B: No, he __doesn't__ . He __goes to school at 8:00__ .

2 A: Does Tom go to bed at 11?

 B: _____ , he _____ . He _____ .

3 A: Do you swim every day?

 B: _____ , I _____ . I _____ .

Sat., Sun.

4 A: Do Steve and David play tennis in the afternoon?

 B: _____ , they _____ .

What Does She Do?

⭐ Catch the grammar

Look and speak. Choose the right ones.

Ⓐ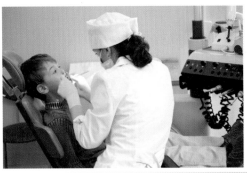

Ⓑ

A: **What** is she?

   Is she a scientist?

B: No, she is not a scientist.

   She is a (dentist / nurse).

A: **What** is he?

   Is he a policeman?

B: No, he is not a policeman.

   He is a (mailman / firefighter).

A: **What** does a dentist do?

   Does a dentist clean our teeth?

B: Yes, a dentist cleans our teeth.

A: **What** does she say?

B: "Brush your teeth every day!"

A: **What** does he do?

   Does he deliver the mail?

B: Yes, he does.

A: **What** does he say?

B: "Here is a parcel for you."

⭐ Make it yours

1. Be/Common Verb Question

Be-verb Question	Common Verb Question
Am I ~?	Do I like ~?
Are you (they/we) ~?	Do you (they/we) ~?
Is he (she/it) ~?	Does he (she/it) ~?

Ⓒ

Ⓓ

A: **What** are you?

  Are you a soldier?

B: No, I'm not.

  I am a (soldier / driver).

A: **What** are they?

  Are they singers?

B: No, they are not.

  They are (lifeguards / policemen).

A: **What** do you do?

  Do you drive a taxi?

B: Yes, I do.

A: **What** do you say?

B: "Buckle your seatbelts."

A: **What** do they do?

  Do they save people in the sea?

B: Yes, they save people.

A: **What** do they say?

B: "Don't dive in there."

2. Wh-question

What + Be-verb ~?	What + do/does ~ Common Verb ~?
What are you ~?	**What** do you ~?
What are they ~?	**What** do they ~?
What is he/she ~?	**What** does he/she ~?
What is it ~?	**What** does it ~?

Exercise

A Choose the right ones.

1 (Is / Are) the horse in the barn?

→ Yes, it (is / isn't / aren't).

(Does / Do) the horse eat bugs?

→ No, it (does / does not / don't).

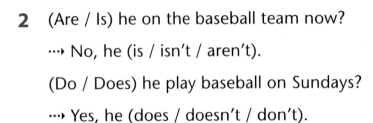

2 (Are / Is) he on the baseball team now?

→ No, he (is / isn't / aren't).

(Do / Does) he play baseball on Sundays?

→ Yes, he (does / doesn't / don't).

3 (Are / Is) they in the library now?

→ Yes, they (are / is / aren't).

(Do / Does) they go to the library every day?

→ No, they (do / don't / doesn't).

4 (Are / Is) you thirsty?

→ (Yes / No), I (am / isn't / do).

(Do / Does) you like cold water?

→ (Yes / No), I (do / don't / am).

B Unscramble.

1 the computer game / you / do / like _____ ?

2 what / the firefighter / does / do _____ ?

3 does / what / the policeman / do _____ ?

4 she / does / like / the shoes _____ ?

C **Make wh-questions by filling in the blanks.**

1　The rabbit eats grass.　　···▸　What ___does___ the rabbit ___eat___ ?

2　The monkey likes bananas. ···▸ What _____ the monkey _____ ?

3　She drinks orange juice.　···▸　What _____ she _____ ?

4　I eat a chocolate cake on ···▸ What _____ you _____ on your
　　my birthday.　　　　　　　birthday?

D **Answer the questions.**

Tom's Hobbies

In the spring — catch the fish

In the summer — swim in the sea

In the fall — climb the mountain

In the winter — go skating

1　Does Tom catch fish in the spring?　_____ , _____ _____ .

2　What does Tom do in the summer?　_____ _____ in the sea.

3　Does Tom go skating in the fall?　_____ , _____ _____ .

4　What does Tom do in the fall?　_____ _____ _____ _____ .

5　What does Tom do in the winter?　_____ _____ _____ .

What Do You Have?

⭐ Catch the grammar

Look and speak.

A I **have** a book.

You **have** a book, too.

But they **have** notebooks.

I   you   they

B The kangaroo **has** a long tail.

But the pig **has** a short tail.

kangaroo   pig

C The bird **has** wings.

But the rabbit **does not have** wings.

I **don't have** wings either.

The rabbit **has** long ears.

But the bird **does not have** long ears.

I **don't have** long ears either.

bird

rabbit   I

⭐ Make it yours

1. Have / Has

Affirmative	Negative
I (You / We / They) have it.	I (You / We / They) don't have it.
He (She / It) has it.	He (She / It) doesn't have it.

> **Grammar Point**   Have / Has (to hold, possess, or experience)
>
> 1. **Have:** I, you, we, they, **Has:** he, she, it
>
> 2. **What do/does ~ have?**

Check the right ones.

Do you **have** a bike?

☐ Yes, I **do**. I have a bike.

☐ No, I **don't**.

   I **don't have** a bike.

Does she **have** a cold?

☐ Yes, she **does**. She has a cold.

☐ No, she **doesn't**.

   She **doesn't have** a cold.

  What **do** you **have** in your bedroom?

   ⋯▶ I **have** a bed and a desk.

  What **does** she **have** in her drawer?

   ⋯▶ She **has** two pens and one eraser.

2. What do/does ~ have?

Question	Answer
What do I (you / they / we) have?	I have ~
What does he (she / it) have?	He has ~

Exercise

 Choose the right ones.

1 Sarah (have / has) many pencils in her pencil case.

⋯▸ Does she (have / has) many pencils in her pencil case?

- -

2 The elephant (have / has) large ears.

⋯▸ Does the elephant (have / has) large ears?

- -

3 I (have / has) a computer in my room.

⋯▸ Do you (have / has) a computer in your room?

- -

4 The cars (have / has) four wheels.

⋯▸ Do the cars (have / has) four wheels?

Cross out the wrong ones in the pictures.

1

You have many toy cars.

But you do not have a toy robot.

2

I have many music CDs.

But I do not have audiotapes.

3

He has frogs.

But he does not have a tadpole.

4

She has blue ribbons.

But she does not have a red ribbon.

ⓒ Fill in the blanks.

1 The bird has two wings.

But the frog _____ _____ two wings.

- -

2 The deer have horns.

But the lions _____ _____ horns.

- -

3 We have black hair.

But they _____ _____ black hair.

ⓓ Answer the questions.

Name	8:00 ~ 9:00	9:00 ~ 10:00	10:00 ~ 11:00
Tom	Math	English	Science
Judy	English	Science	Math
Sarah and Brian	Science	Math	English

1 A: Does Tom have a science class at 9:00?

B: No, he _____. He doesn't _____ a science class at 9:00.

He _____ a science class at 10:00.

2 A: Do Sarah and Brian have a math class at 8:00?

B: _____, they _____. They _____ _____ a math class at 8:00.

They _____ a math class at 9:00.

3 A: Does Judy have an English class at 10:00?

B: _____, she _____. She _____ _____ an English class at 10:00.

She _____ an English class at 8:00.

Chapter 2 Review Test

A Choose the right ones.

1   (Is / Are) they your friends?

2   (Is / Are) she at school now?

3   (Do / Does) you know her name?

4   (Do / Does) she know your name?

5   (Do / Does) the bears swim in the winter?

6   (Do / Does) the dog sleep in its house?

7   Does the turtle (live / lives) in the sea?

8   Do you (swim / swims) every Saturday?

9   Does the tree (have / has) leaves?

10   Do they (have / has) a new video game?

B Fill in the blanks.

1   A: Is the tall man a teacher?

   B: Yes, he _____.

2   A: Does the teacher have a cold?

   B: Yes, he _____.

3   A: Do the students have backpacks?

   B: _____, they _____.

teacher   Susan   Emily   Tom

4   A: Does Susan have a radio?

   B: No, she _____.

   She _____ a camera.

5   A: What do Emily and Tom have?

   B: They _____ a basket.

44

C Write contractions.

1 She does not eat candies. = She _____ eat candies.

2 They do not like the movie. = They _____ like the movie.

D Answer the questions.

	Morning	Afternoon	Evening	Night	
	7:00	12:00	7:00	9:00	11:00
Tom	go to school	swim	eat	sleep	
Mrs. Kim	is busy / work at the bank		exercise	eat	sleep
Steve and David	work in the market	play tennis	eat	study	sleep

1 Is Mrs. Kim busy in the morning? _____

2 What does Tom do in the afternoon? _____

3 What does Tom do at 9 p.m.? _____

4 What does Mrs. Kim do at 7 p.m.? _____

5 What do Steve and David do in the morning?

_____

6 Do Steve and David go to bed at 9 p.m.? _____

7 What do Steve and David do in the afternoon?

_____

8 Does Mrs. Kim eat at 9 p.m.? _____

Challenge Test

A ▶ Make questions and then answer the questions.

1

The giraffe eats worms.

Q: Does the giraffe eat worms?

A: No, it does not .

2

The whale lives in the desert.

Q: _____?

A: _____ .

3

The crocodile has a short tail.

Q: _____?

A: _____ .

4

Tom's parents have sunglasses.

Q: _____?

A: _____ .

B ▶ Guess what it is!

1 I have this.
My brother and sister have this, too.
But my parents do not have this.

❓ What is "this"? _____

2 My sister has this, but my brother
does not have this. My parents have this.

❓ What is "this"? _____

My things	comic books, potato chips, baseball, glove, music CD
Brother's things	comic books, music CD, chocolate, jelly
Sister's things	math books, jelly, music CD
Parents' things	comic books, math books, popcorn

C ▶ **Find the wrong ones.**

1   My friends has many books.
         have

2   Susan do not have black hair.

3   You does not have black hair.

4   She does not has a bike.

5   I do not has a sister.

6   What does you do at church?

7   They doesn't like the movie.

8   She does not plays football.

D ▶ **Fill in the blanks.**

1   A: __Is__ the fish in the bowl? (**be**)

    B: Yes, __it__ __is__ .

2   A: _____ they singers? (**be**)

    B: _____, they _____.

3   A: _____ she _____ breakfast at 8 a.m.? (**eat**)

    B: _____, she _____.

4   A: _____ he _____ a blue necktie? (**have**)

    B: _____, he _____.

5   A: _____ the cats _____ short tails? (**have**)

    B: No, they _____.

Chapter 3

1. Adjective + singular noun

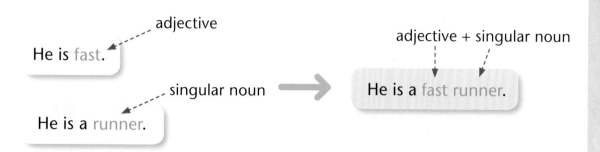

He is fast. ← adjective

He is a runner. ← singular noun

→ adjective + singular noun

He is a fast runner.

2. Adjective + plural noun

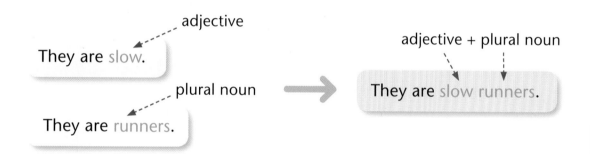

They are slow. ← adjective

They are runners. ← plural noun

→ adjective + plural noun

They are slow runners.

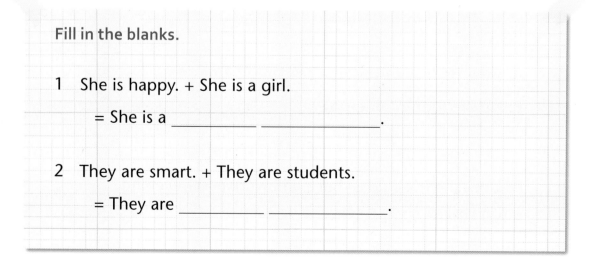

Fill in the blanks.

1 She is happy. + She is a girl.

= She is a _____ _____.

2 They are smart. + They are students.

= They are _____ _____.

He Sleeps Quietly.

⭐ Ⅰ Catch the grammar

Look and speak.

Ⓐ The baby is <u>quiet</u>.

The baby sleeps **quietly** at night.

Does Dad sleep **quietly**?

No, he is <u>loud</u>. He sleeps **loudly** every night.

Ⓑ Jane is <u>beautiful</u>.

She sings **beautifully** every day.

Does Mom sing **beautifully**, too?

No, she is very <u>noisy</u>. She sings **noisily**.

Ⓒ The cow cries, "Moo," and the dog cries, "Bark! Bark!" Their sounds are <u>different</u>.

They cry **differently**.

⭐ 2 Make it yours

1. Adverb = Adjective + -ly

Adverb	Adjective
I smile happily.	I am happy.
You talk quietly.	You are a quiet boy.
He plays badly.	He is a bad player.
She talks slowly.	She is a slow talker.

* beautifully
interestingly
quickly
poorly

Grammar Point Adverb (describing the common verb)

1. **Adverb = Adjective + -ly** (happy – happily)
2. **Adverb = Adjective** (fast – fast)
3. **Adverb ≠ Adjective** (good – well)

D He is <u>late</u> for school every day.

Does he go to sleep **late** every day?

Yes, he goes to sleep **late**.

No, he does not go to sleep **late**. He goes to sleep early.

E Tom is a <u>fast</u> runner.

Does Emily run **fast**, too?

Yes, she runs **fast**.

No, she does not run **fast**. She runs slowly.

F They are <u>good</u> guitar players.

Do they play the piano **well**, too?

Yes, they play **well**.

No, they do not play **well**.

---

2. Adverb = Adjective

Adverb	Adjective
It flies fast.	The plane is fast.
He comes late.	He is late.
He works hard.	He is a hard worker.

3. Adverb ≠ Adjective

Adverb	Adjective
He can draw well.	He is a good drawer.

Exercise

 Change the adjectives into adverbs.

Adjective	Adverb
1 a quiet boy	He sings _____.
2 a noisy boy	He cries _____.
3 a beautiful girl	She sings _____.
4 a happy girl	She laughs _____.
5 a fast boy	He runs _____.
6 a hard worker	He works _____.
7 a late bus	The bus comes _____.
8 a slow turtle	It walks _____.
9 a good singer	She sings _____.

B Choose the right ones.

1 He plays the game (quiet / quietly).
   He is a (quiet / quietly) player.

2 She is (sad / sadly).
   She cries (sad / sadly).

3 The dog is (angry / angrily).
   It barks (angry / angrily).

4 He is a (slow / slowly) reader.
   He reads (slow / slowly).

5 The train is (late / lately).
   The train comes (late / lately)
   every morning.

6 They dance (beautiful / beautifully).
   They are (beautiful / beautifully)
   dancers.

C Fill in the blanks.

1 The car is a fast car.

   It runs _____.

2 Jason is a good painter.

   He paints _____.

3 He is late for school every day.

   He comes to school _____ every day.

4 Jane has a beautiful smile.

   She smiles _____.

D Correct the underlined words.

My friend is special to me. He uses a wheelchair.

So he plays sports poor[1].

But he sings beautiful[2], and he is very kindly[3].

He does not speak angrily.

He talks to people kind[4].

Also, he plays the piano wonderfully.

He makes paper ships quick[5], too.

He is fastly[6]. He makes everything fast.

He is very smart. I like my special friend.

1 _____   2 _____

3 _____   4 _____

5 _____   6 _____

The Bird Can Fly.

⭐ Catch the grammar

Read and choose the right answers.

How are they different?	
fly	The bird **can** fly. The fish **cannot** fly.
swim	The bird **cannot** live in the water. The fish **can** live in the water.
hop	The bird **can** hop. The fish **cannot** hop.
sing	The bird **can** sing. The fish **cannot** sing.

1 **Can** the fish hop?   ☐ Yes, it can.   ☑ No, it cannot.

2 **Can** the bird fly in the sky?   ☐ Yes, it can.   ☐ No, it cannot.

3 **Can** the fish sing?   ☐ Yes, it can.   ☐ No, it cannot.

4 **Can** the bird hop?   ☐ Yes, it can.   ☐ No, it cannot.

⭐ Make it yours

1. Can (Ability, Permission)

Subject + can + Verb ~	
Affirmative	She can run fast. (She can runs.(**X**))
Negative	She cannot run fast. (She cannot runs.(**X**))

* Contraction: cannot = can't

Check the right answers.

1   **Can** the turtle run fast?

☐ Yes, it can.
☐ No, it cannot.

2   Can she sing a song well?

☐ Yes, she can.
☐ No, she cannot.

3   Can your mom cook well?

☐ Yes, she can.
☐ No, she cannot.

4   Can you write quickly?

☐ Yes, I can.
☐ No, I cannot.

5   Eric: **Can I** play a computer game now?

Mom: ☐ Yes, you can. / ☐ No, you cannot.

Play with your brother.

6   Judy: **Can I** watch TV now?

Mom: ☐ Yes, you can. / ☐ No, you cannot.

Go to bed now. It is too late.

2. Question / Answer

	Question	Answer
Ability	Can you run fast?	Yes, I can. / No, I cannot.
Permission	Can I watch TV now?	Yes, you can. / No, you cannot.

3 Exercise

A Choose the right ones.

1 The butterfly (can / cannot) fly.

The snake (can / cannot) fly.

2 The dog (can / cannot) run.

The bat (can / cannot) run.

3 The kangaroo (can / cannot) swim.

The fish (can / cannot) swim.

4 The ant (can / cannot) jump.

The kangaroo (can / cannot) jump.

B Check the right answers.

1

Cindy: Can I talk to Judy now?

Mom: _____.

She is sick now.

☐ Yes, you can.

☐ No, you cannot.

2

Boy: Can I sit here?

Man: _____.

It is wet.

☐ Yes, you can.

☐ No, you cannot.

C Answer the questions.

1 Can she play the piano?

⋯▶ Yes, _____ _____.

2 Can the ant fly?

⋯▶ _____, _____ _____.

3 Can you swim?

⋯▶ Yes, _____ _____.

4 Can they jump?

⋯▶ _____, _____ _____.

D Check all the right ones.

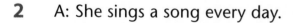

- ☐ Dad can see the elephant.
- ☐ Mom can see the elephant.
- ☐ The baby cannot see the elephant.
- ☐ Kevin cannot see the elephant.

- ☐ My sister cannot swim well.
- ☐ My brother can swim well.
- ☐ My grandfather can swim well.
- ☐ My dad cannot swim well.

E Fill in the blanks.

1 A: They are good cooks.

B: Can they cook pizza well?

A: _____, they _____.

2 A: She sings a song every day.

B: _____ _____ _____ a song beautifully?

A: _____, she _____.

3 A: My sister is a dancer.

B: _____ _____ _____ well?

A: _____, she _____.

4 A: My dad rides a bicycle every day.

B: _____ _____ _____ a bicycle well?

A: _____, he _____.

You Must Go Now.

1 Catch the grammar

Read and put the right numbers.

1 You **must** stop here.
  You **must not** go.

2 You **must** turn right.
  You **must not** turn left.

3 You **must** walk.
  You **must not** run.

4 You **must not** swim here.
  You **must** swim in the swimming pool.

Don't talk. This is a library.
You **must not** talk here.

2 Make it yours

1. Must (law, order)

Affirmative	You must go. (must goes(**X**))
Negative	You must not go.

* Contraction: must not = musn't
* Question: Do I **have to** go?
  Answer: Yes, you **have to** go. / No, you don't **have to** go.

> **Grammar Point** Must / Should
>
> 1. **Must:** law, order
>
> 2. **Should:** idea, suggestion

Match.

Don't cross the street.
It is not safe now.

•   •

You **must** swim in the pool.
You **must not** swim in the river.

Don't swim in the river.
It is deep.

•   •

You **must** wait here.
You **must not** cross the street.

- -

Read and speak.

1   A: Mom, I am sleepy.

   B: You **should** sleep now.

2   A: Can I eat the cookies?

   B: Yes, you can. But you **must not** eat the
      cookies in the basket. They are for the dog.
      You **should** have the cookies in the jar.

2. Should (idea, suggestion)

Affirmative	You should sleep. (should sleeps(**X**))
Negative	You should not sleep.
Question	Should I sleep?
Answer	Yes, you should sleep. / No, you should not sleep.

* Contraction: should not = shouldn't

3 Exercise

 A **What do the signs say? Choose the right ones.**

1 You (must / must not) watch out.

2 You (must / must not) dive.

3 You (must / must not) talk.

4 You (must / must not) cross now.

B **Choose the right ones.**

1

 : I am sick.

(Should / Must) I see a doctor?

 : Yes, you should.

2

 : I am hungry.

 : You (should / must) eat some bread.

3

 : Can I play a computer game?

 : No, you can't.

_____

4

 : Can I eat the cake now?

 : No, you can't.

_____

☐ You must do your homework now.

☐ You can play a computer game.

☐ You must not do your homework now.

☐ You must eat cake.

☐ You should clean your hands, first.

☐ You can eat the cake.

C Correct the wrong ones.

1 She must ~~leaves~~ now.
leave

2 They not must sleep here.

3 You should drinks water now.

4 I shouldnt eat the banana.

5 Should she sleeps now?

6 They must wears skates on the ice.

7 He should does his homework now.

D Choose the right ones and fill in the blanks.

1 She does not brush her teeth every day.

Brush your teeth every day.

= You (can / should) _____ your teeth every day.

2 My sister eats many candies every day.

Don't eat many candies every day.

= You (cannot / should not) _____ many candies every day.

3 My brother does not wash his feet well.

Wash your feet well.

= You (can / should) _____ your feet well.

4 They do not study every day.

Study every day.

= You (can / should) _____ every day.

Review Test

A Choose the right ones.

1   The baby is (loud / loudly).

   The baby cries (loud / loudly) every night.

2   They are (good / well) basketball players.

   They play basketball (good / well).

3   My sister is a (happy / happily) singer.

   She sings (happy / happily).

4   I am a (quiet / quietly) talker.

   I talk (quiet / quietly).

B Fill in the blanks.

1

   A: Can the baby walk fast?

   B: [____] , [_____] [_____] .

2

   A: Can you eat this?

   B: [____] , [_____] [_____] .

3

   A: Can she ride this bike?

   B: [____] , [_____] [_____] .

4

   A: Can I drink the water?

   B: [____] , [_____] [_____] [_____] .

C Make the questions and the negatives.

1   The boy can play baseball.

    Question   _____ _____ _____ play baseball?

    Negative   The boy _____ play baseball.

2   Sally can open the letter.

    Question   _____ _____ open the letter?

    Negative   Sally _____ open the letter.

3   I should sleep now.

    Question   _____ _____ sleep now?

    Negative   I _____ _____ sleep now.

D Unscramble.

1   the chicken / fly / cannot / in the sky   _____ .

2   can / study / they / in the library   _____ ?

3   can / I / a picture / draw / now   _____ .

4   they / study / hard / must   _____ .

E Fill in the blanks.

1   Jim: Can I use this pen?

    Tim: _____

        Don't use the pen.

    ☐ Yes, you can.
    ☐ No, you cannot.

2   Ben: Can I eat this apple?

    David: _____

        Eat the red apple, too.

    ☐ Yes, you can.
    ☐ No, you cannot.

Challenge Test

A ▶ **Fill in the blanks.**

1 She is a beautiful dancer.

⋯▸ She dances _____.

2 The train is fast.

⋯▸ It runs _____.

3 The kitten is noisy.

⋯▸ It cries _____.

4 I am a good violinist.

⋯▸ I play the violin _____.

B ▶ **Unscramble and match the right ones.**

1 must / not / you / run

_____.

•   • Don't watch TV now.

2 TV / not / you / should / watch

_____.

•   • Don't eat many candies.

3 should / many candies / not / you / eat

_____.

•   • Don't run!

C ▶ **Guess what it is and fill in the blanks.**

1 It cannot walk fast.
It can live in the sea.
It is a _____.

2 It cannot jump on the ground.
It can fly.
It is a _____.

bird   snail   lion   turtle

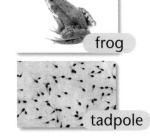

frog   dragonfl   tadpole   hippo

D ▶ Choose the right ones.

1

I [play / am] happy.

2

She [is / talks] loudly.

3

They [are / eat] quiet.

4

They [are / dance] beautiful.

E ▶ Correct the wrong ones.

1 The boy talks ~~quiet~~.
   quietly

2 She smiles happy.

3 Bats cannot see good.

4 The fish can lives in the sea.

5 You must sleeps now.

6 Does he can go now?

F ▶ Choose the wrong ones.

1

She is
① every day.
② happy.
③ fast.

2

He eats
① donuts.
② slow.
③ slowly.

3

She makes
① cookies quickly.
② cookies happy.
③ cookies well.

4

I am
① happy.
② happily.
③ a student.

5

They sing
① every day.
② happy.
③ fast.

6

You swim
① fast.
② good.
③ well.

Chapter 4

Quick Check

1. Be-verb

Subject + Be-verb	Question	Wh-question
I am ~.	Am I ~?	What am I?
You are ~.	Are you ~?	Who are you?
He / She is ~.	Is he/she ~?	How is he/she?
It is ~.	Is it ~?	How is it?
They/We are ~.	Are they/we ~?	How are they/we?

2. Common verb

	Common Verb	Question	Wh-question
I You They We	like study put catch	Do I like ~? Do you like ~? Do they like ~? Do we like ~?	What do I like? What do you like? What do they like? What do we like?
He She It	likes studies puts catches	Does he like ~? Does she like ~? Does it like ~?	What does he like? What does she like? What does it like?

Make questions.

1. They run every day. ⋯➡ _____?
2. She runs every day. ⋯➡ _____?

What / Who / Which

 Catch the grammar

Read and circle the right pictures.

A A: Is this a cheese pizza?

B: No, it isn't.

A: **What** is it?

B: It is a pepperoni pizza.

B A: Do you like yogurt?

B: No, I do not like yogurt.

A: **What** do you like?

B: I like ice cream.

A: **What ice cream** do you like?

B: I like strawberry ice cream.

C A: Is the tall boy Steve?

B: No, he isn't.

A: **Who** is he?

B: He is Jim.

 Make it yours

1. What (about things) / Who (about persons)

	Question	Answer
What	What do you eat for a snack?	I eat cookies.
	What cookies do you eat?	I eat chocolate cookies.
Who	Who(Whom) do you like?	I like Jane.

Grammar Point   What / Who / Which

1. **What:** asking about things
2. **Who:** asking about person
3. **Which + noun ~, A or B?:** asking for a choice

D A: Do you like Susan?

B: No, I do not like tall girls.

A: **Who (Whom)** do you like?

B: I like Judy. She is not tall.

E A: **What** do you need?

B: I need a hat.

A: **Which hat** do you need, the party hat **or** the round hat?

B: I need the round hat.

F A: **Which fruit** do you like, bananas **or** apples?

B: I like apples.

G A: **Which apples** do you like, red apples **or** green apples?

B: I like both.

2. Which (for a choice)

Which + Noun ~, A or B? (for a choice)	Answer
Which one do you need, A or B?	I need B.
Which do you need, A or B?	I need A and B. (= I need both.)

* Which hat = What hat = What kind of hat

69

Exercise

A **Choose the right ones.**

Question	Answer
1 (Who / What) do you like?	I like Jason.
2 (What / Who) does he eat for lunch?	He eats a sandwich.
3 (Who / Which) do they want, orange juice or milk?	They want milk.
4 (What / Who) color does Steve like?	He likes purple.
5 (Who / Which) pencil does she like, the long or the short one?	She likes the long one.
6 (Who / Which) are you?	I am Judy Lee.

B **Fill in the blanks.**

1 A: Which one _____ she need, a fork or a spoon?

B: She needs a _____.

2 A: Which one _____ the boy need, boots or an umbrella?

B: He needs boots _____ an umbrella.

3 A: Which one _____ you need, chopsticks or a fork?

B: I need _____.

4 A: There are cats.

_____ cat do you like, the black cat _____ the white cat?

B: I like both.

C Answer the questions.

	Susan	My Brother and I	My Sister
Favorite Pets	a dog	a cat	a bird
Favorite Fruits	bananas	grapes	apples

1 Which pet does Susan like?

_____

2 Which fruit do my brother and I like?

_____

3 Which fruit does my sister like?

_____

4 Which pet does my sister like?

_____

D Unscramble.

1 you / do / what / eat / in the morning

_____ ?

2 coffee / or / which / she / does / like / milk

_____ ?

3 he / does / like / grapes / or / fruit / oranges / which

_____ ?

2   Where / When

⭐ **Catch the grammar**

Check Tom's monthly schedule and fill in the blanks.

A   **Where** does Tom go every Friday?

⟶ He goes **to** the swimming pool.

Where does Tom go every Saturday?

⟶ He goes **to** the _____.

swimming pool   library

B   **Where** is he in the morning?

⟶ He is **at** school.

Where does he study in the afternoon?

⟶ He studies **at** home.

Where does he swim in the afternoon?

⟶ He swims **in** _____.

	Study	Swim
In the morning	at school	-
In the afternoon	at home	in the swimming pool

⭐ **Make it yours**

1. Where (about places)

Question	Answer
Where do you study?	In the room.
Where do they study?	At home. / At school.
Where does she go?	To the library.
Where does he sleep?	In the bed.

Grammar Point   Where / When, Preposition

1. **Where:** asking about places (in, at, to, on)

2. **When:** asking about time (in, at, on)

C

Morning		Afternoon	
1st Movie	9:00	4th Movie	2:00
2nd Movie	10:30	5th Movie	3:30
3rd Movie	12:00	6th Movie	5:00

When(= What time) does the first movie start in the morning?

···▸ It starts **at** 9:00 **in** the morning.

When(= What time) does the fourth movie start in the afternoon?

···▸ It starts _____ **in** the afternoon.

D **When**(= What date) does he have a swimming class?

···▸ He has it **on** October 4.

When(= What day) does he go to the library?

···▸ He goes to the library every _____.

swimming class   piano   library

2. When (about time, day, date, season)

Question	Answer
When **do** you swim?	In the afternoon. / In the summer.
When **does** she eat?	At noon. / At night. / At 12:00.
When **does** he have a party?	On Monday. [day] / On July 2. [date] / On Christmas Day.

* Every Saturday = on Saturdays

3 Exercise

A Choose the right ones.

Question	Answer
1 (Where / When) do you go on Sundays?	I go to church.
2 (Where / When) do you eat dinner?	We eat at 7:00.
3 (Where / When) can we go to the camp?	You can go on Saturday.
4 (Where / When) do you get snow?	We get snow in the winter.

B Match the right ones.

1 Where do you play?   •   • I play on Sundays.

2 When do you play?   •   • We eat at home.

3 When do you eat dinner?   •   • I play on the playground.

4 When do you go to the library? •   • We eat at 6:00.

5 Where do you eat dinner on your •   • I go there on Tuesday.
   birthday?

C Choose the right ones.

1 A: When do you eat the snacks?

   B: We eat (at / on / in) noon.

2 A: Where does the bat live?

   B: It lives (at / on / in) the cave.

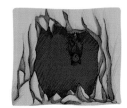

3 A: Where do you study?

   B: I study (at / on / in) home.

4 A: When does the rooster crow?

   B: It crows (at / on / in) the morning.

- -

5 A: When does Kevin have a swimming class?

   B: Kevin has a swimming class (at / on / in) Tuesdays.

swimming class

- -

6 A: When does Susan's art class start?

   B: It starts (at / on / in) May 18.

Art class starts.

D **Answer the questions.**

The bears cannot find food in the winter.
So, the bears sleep for a long time in the winter.

They sleep in caves.
They don't come out in the winter.

They eat and eat in the summer and fall
and sleep for many weeks in the cold winter.
Then, they wake up in the spring again.

1 Where do the bears sleep? _____

2 When do they wake up? _____

3 When do they eat a lot? _____

4 When do they sleep for a long time? _____

How Does It Taste?

⭐ Catch the grammar

Read and circle the right ones.

1 **How** does it taste?

⋯▸ The cake <u>tastes</u> sweet.

⋯▸ It <u>tastes like</u> chocolate.

2 **How** does it look?

⋯▸ The dog <u>looks</u> ugly.

⋯▸ It <u>looks like</u> a gorilla.

3 **How** do they smell?

⋯▸ The shoes <u>smell</u> bad!

⋯▸ They <u>smell like</u> cheese.

4 **How** does it feel?

⋯▸ The pillow <u>feels</u> soft.

⋯▸ It <u>feels like</u> cotton.

⭐ Make it yours

1. How does it ~?

How do/does + Subject + Verb?	Subject + Verb + Adjective.
How does it taste?	It tastes good.
How does it smell?	It smells bad.
How do they look?	They look beautiful.
How do they feel?	They feel soft.

Grammar Point Wh-question with Linking Verb

1. **How does it taste? / It tastes + adjective.**

2. **What does it taste like? / It tastes like + noun.**

Guess what it is? Fill in the blanks.

clock

eraser

sandwich

1 A: Does it <u>look like</u> a triangle?

B: No, it doesn't.

A: **What** does it <u>look like</u>?

B: It <u>looks like</u> a circle.

A: Oh, it is a _____.

2 A: Does it <u>look like</u> a circle?

B: No, it doesn't.

A: **What** does it <u>look like</u>?

B: It <u>looks like</u> a rectangle.

A: Oh, it is an _____.

3 A: Does it <u>look like</u> a rectangle?

B: No, it doesn't.

A: **What** does it <u>look like</u>?

B: It <u>looks like</u> a triangle.

A: Oh, it is a _____.

2. What does it ~ like?

What do/does + Subject + Verb + like?	Subject + Verb + like + Noun.
What does it taste like?	It tastes like cake.
What does it smell like?	It smells like chicken soup.
What does it look like?	It looks like a lion.
What does it feel like?	It feels like cotton.

Exercise

A Choose the right ones.

1 A: How does it feel?

   B: It feels (soft / a soft pillow).

2 A: What does it feel like?

   B: It feels like (soft / a soft pillow).

3 A: How do I look?

   B: You look (pretty / a princess).

4 A: What do I look like?

   B: You look like (pretty / a princess).

5 A: How does it taste?

   B: It tastes (spicy / a hot
   pepper).

6 A: What does it taste like?

   B: It tastes like (spicy / a hot
   pepper).

7 A: (How / What) does it smell?

   B: It smells sweet!

8 A: (How / What) does it smell like?

   B: It smells like popcorn.

B Put the right numbers in the blanks.

① happy   ② soft   ③ angry   ④ rough   ⑤ sad   ⑥ bumpy

How does this feel?

1 It feels _____.

2 It feels _____.

3 It feels _____.

How do they feel now?

4 The frogs feel _____.

5 They feel _____.

6 They feel _____.

C Match the right ones.

1   How does it taste?   •   •   It tastes sweet.

2   How does she feel?   •   •   They look like sisters.

3   How do I look?   •   •   It smells like coffee.

4   What does it smell like?   •   •   She feels sick.

5   What do they look like?   •   •   You look pretty.

D Unscramble.

1   does / how / this / taste   _____ ?

2   looks / beautiful / she   _____ .

3   like / look / they / roses   _____ .

4   what / the food / does / smell / like   _____ ?

E Answer the questions.

1   A: Does Tom look happy?

    B: Yes, he _____ happy.
      He looks _____ a happy boy.

2   A: Does the dog look _____ a gorilla?

    B: No, it does not _____ _____ a gorilla.

3   A: Does it taste spicy?

    B: Yes, it _____ spicy.
      It _____ _____ a spicy pepper.

Review Test

A Choose the right ones.

1 (What / Who) does she like? — She likes roses.

2 (Which / Who) one does he have, a pen or an eraser? — He has a pen.

3 (What / Who) do you like? — I like my English teacher.

4 (Where / How) do you go on Sundays? — I go to church.

5 (Where / When / How) do you go to the mountains?

　　　　　　　　　　　— I go to the mountains on Saturdays.

6 (When / How) does it feel? — It feels cold.

7 (Where / What / How) does it look like? — It looks like a gorilla.

8 (Where / How / What) do they look? — They look sad!

9 (Where / How / When) do you play after school? — I play on the playground.

B Fill in the blanks.

1 A: Where do you live?

　　B: I live _____ Seoul.

2 A: When do you go to church?

　　B: I go to church _____ Sundays.

3 A: When do you have the birthday party?

　　B: We have the party _____ noon.

Word Bank　at　on　in

4   A: Where do you study?

      B: I study _____ home.

5   A: When do you go to the swimming pool?

      B: I go to the swimming pool _____ Saturdays.

C Unscramble.

1	does / how / taste/ it	?
2	he / strong / looks	.
3	like / who / she / does	?
4	you / do / sit / where / in this class	?
5	do / swim / when / you	?

D Answer the questions.

teacher   Jane

1   A: How does the teacher look?

      B: He _____ _____.

2   A: How does the fat boy look?

      B: He _____ _____.

3   A: How does Jane look?

      B: She _____ happy.

4   A: What does the dog look like?

Word Bank   tired   hungry   gorilla   B: It _____ _____ a _____.

Challenge Test

A ▶ Fill in the blanks.

1 _____ _____ you want, orange juice _____ milk?

2 _____ _____ you feel now? — I feel hot!

3 _____ _____ he study? — He studies in the bedroom.

4 _____ _____ they leave? — They leave on Friday.

5 _____ _____ you study? — I study in the library.

6 _____ _____ it look like? — It looks like a squirrel.

7 _____ _____ she look? — She looks tired.

8 _____ _____ she study at home? — She studies English.

9 _____ _____ he do in the library? — He reads many books.

10 _____ _____ you like? — I like the teacher. He is very kind.

11 _____ _____ you play after school? — I play football.

12 _____ _____ he like for lunch? — He likes a chicken sandwich.

B ▶ Answer the questions.

1 A: What time does Tom go to sleep?

B: He _____ .

2 A: What day does Jason play football?

B: _____ .

3 A: What date is John at the gym?

B: _____ .

4 A: What time does Jason watch TV?

B: _____ .

C Correct the wrong ones.

1 When does she like for breakfast? — She likes bread.
   What

2 Which one is the new bike, the green one and the brown one?

3 What do you have the party? — On January 12.

4 What student do you know? — I know the tall girl. She is Jane.

5 How does it looks like? — It looks like a dog.

D Answer the questions.

Steve likes fruit.
His favorite fruit is grapes.

orange   grapes   apple   bananas   kiwi   watermelon

Tom likes meat. His favorite meat is chicken.

pork   chicken   beef

Emily likes vegetables. Her favorite vegetable is broccoli.

cabbage   onion   green pepper   broccoli   carrot

1 Which one is Tom's favorite meat? _____

2 Which one is Emily's favorite vegetable? _____

What do you like? Choose and write.

3 Which fruit do you like? _____

4 Which meat do you like? _____

5 Which vegetable do you like? _____

Chapter 5

Possessives

Subjective Pronoun	Possessive
I am Tom.	It is **my** dog.
You are a doctor.	This is **your** cat.
He is a policeman.	This is **his** gun.
She is a good cook.	This is **her** apron.
It is a cute dog.	This is **its** house.
They are my friends.	It is **their** dog.
We are doctors.	This is **our** hospital.

Choose the right ones.

They are (his / her) glasses.

This is (his / her) hat.

This is (his / her) bag.

Me / You / Him / Her / Them / Us / It

 Catch the grammar

Look and speak.

1

I	like	you	.
You	like	me	, too.

2

We	like	you	.
You	like	us	, too.

3

Hi, Betty.   Hi, Jason.

Jason	knows	Betty	.
He	knows	her	.
She	knows	him	, too.

4

Jason	likes	the dog	.
He	likes	it	.
It	likes	him	, too.

Grammar Point   Subject and Object Pronouns

1. **I – me, you – you, they – them**

2. **he – him, she – her, we – us, it – it**

5

Susan   Kevin   Judy

Susan   knows   Kevin and Judy .
  ↓   ↓
She   knows   them   .

They   know   her , too.

6

Tim   eats   an apple .
  ↓   ↓
He   likes   it   .

7

Tim and Judy   eat   apples .
      ↓   ↓
   They   like   them   .

⭐ **2 Make it yours**

Pronoun

Subject	Object	Subject	Object
I	me	we	us
you	you	they	them
he	him	it	it
she	her	-	-

3 Exercise

A Choose the right ones.

1 James likes Betty.

   She likes (he / she / him / her), too.

2 I help my brother every day.

   He helps (me / she / him / her), too.

3 You like Alex and Tim.

   (He / She / They) like (you / him), too.

4 Steve eats bananas every day.

   He likes (it / them / they).

5 We like Judy and Sam.

   They like (we / us / they), too.

6 Betty calls James every day.

   He calls (he / she / him / her) every day, too.

B Change the sentences with pronouns.

1 I clean <u>my room</u> every day. = I clean ___it___ every day.

2 I wash <u>my dogs</u> every day. = I wash _____ every day.

3 I like <u>the dog</u>. = I like _____.

4 I help <u>my mom</u> every day. = I help _____ every day.

5 I help <u>my father</u> every day. = I help _____ every day.

6 They know <u>you and me</u>. = They know _____.

C Fill in the blanks.

1

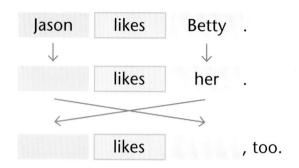

2

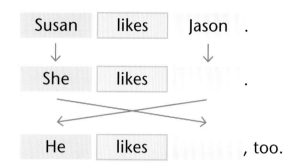

3

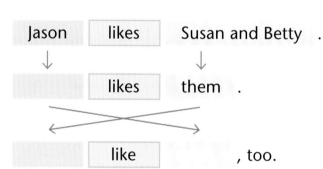

Betty   Susan

Jason

D Fill in the blanks.

1   Do you love ___her___ ?

2   Do you know _____ ?

3   Do you know _____ ?

E Correct the wrong ones.

1   She likes ~~he~~.
        him

2   I know they.

3   He likes I.

4   I like she.

5   Me help her every day.

6   She helps we.

I – My – Me

⭐ Catch the grammar

Read and fill in the blanks.

1
I am a good painter.
Look at **my** picture.
My teacher helps **me** every day.

I – my – me

2
He is a math teacher.
These are **his** students.
His students like **him** very much.

He – [   ] – him

3
She is Judy Lee.
She likes **her** cat.
The cat likes **her**, too.

She – [   ] – her

4
You are a good singer.
I like **your** wonderful song.
I like **you**!

You – [   ] – you

5
My grandparents cook very well.
They cook rice cakes every Sunday.
Their rice cakes are tasty.
I like **them** very much.

They – [   ] – them

6
We are basketball players.
Mr. Kim is **our** team's coach.
He trains **us**.

We – [   ] – us

7   **It** is my cat.
This is **its** house.
I like **it**.

It – [   ] – it

These are my students.
Draw **them**, please!

Sir, it is my cat.
Draw **it**, please!

No, sir! He is my son.
Draw **him**, please!

You are a good painter.
Your pictures are good!
Draw **me** first, please!

Sir, she is my daughter.
Draw **her**, please!

 Make it yours

Subject	Possessive	Object
I am Tom.	I like my teacher.	He likes me.
You are Betty.	I like your bag.	I like you.
He is John.	I like his bike.	I like him.
She is Susan.	I like her sweater.	I like her.
It is Rex.	I like its fur.	I like it.
We are a family.	They like our house.	They like us.
They are my friends.	I like their shoes.	I like them.

3 Exercise

Ⓐ Fill in the blanks.

Subject	Possessive	Object
I	my	me
you		
he		him
she		her
they		
it		it
we		

Ⓑ Choose the right ones.

1 I like my / me dog. The dog likes I / my / me , too.

2 You like you / your dog. The dog likes you / your , too.

3 He likes he / his dog. The dog likes he / his / him , too.

4 She likes she / her dog. The dog likes she / her , too.

5 They like they / their dog. The dog likes they / their / them , too.

6 We like we / our dog. The dog likes we / our / us , too.

7 We like the dog. We like it / its puppy, too.

ⓒ Choose the right ones.

1 She is very beautiful.
Can I draw (she / **her**)?

2 Is this your box?
Can I open (**it** / they / them)?

3 I need (**your** / you) help.
Can I call (your / **you**)?

4 Are these (**your** / you) boxes?
Can I carry (**them** / it / they)?

5 Can (**you** / your) call (I / **me**)?
I need your answer.

6 Look at him.
He is (**my** / me) brother.

7 We are football players.
These are (**our** / we) T-shirts.

8 They are strong.
You need (**their** / them) help.

ⓓ Fill in the blanks.

1 A: Do you like _me_ ? (I)
B: Yes, I like _you_ .

2 A: Does he like _____? (she)
B: Yes, he likes _____.
And she likes _____, too.

3 A: Does she know _____? (he)
B: Yes, she knows _____.
He knows _____, too.

4 A: Do we know _____? (they)
B: Yes, we know _____.
They know _____, too.

5 A: Do they like _____? (it)
B: Yes, they like _____.
It likes _____, too.

6 A: Do I know _____? (you)
B: Yes, you know _____.
I know _____, too.

Whose / Which

⭐1 Catch the grammar

Read and check the right answers.

Jason   Dad   Susan and Judy   teacher

1 Whose cap is this?

☑ This is Jason's cap.

☐ This is Dad's cap.

2 Whose shoes are these?

☐ These are the teacher's shoes.

☐ These are Judy's shoes.

3 **Whose** books are these?

☐ These are Susan and Judy's books.

☐ These are the teacher's books.

⭐2 Make it yours

1. Whose + Noun ~?

Question	Answer
Whose book is this?	This is my book.
	This is Tom's book.
Whose books are these?	These are my parents' books.
	These are Tom and Susan's books.

Grammar Point   Whose / Which

1. **Whose + noun ~?**
2. **Which one(s) ~?**

Read and fill in the blanks.

1   A: **Whose** room is number 1?

 B: It is my parents' room.
  It is very large.

2   A: **Whose** room is number 2?

 B: It is my _____ room.
  It is small.

3   A: **Which** one is your brother's room?

 B: Number _____ is my brother's
  room.

4   A: **Which** one is your grandparents'
  room?

 B: Number _____ is my
  grandparents' room.

2. Which one(s) ~?

Which one(s) + is/are + Possessive + Noun ~?	Answer
Which one is your room?	The messy one is my room.
Which ones are your brother's books?	The big ones are my brother's books.

*One: to avoid the same word (singular)
 Ones: to avoid the same words (plural)

⭐**3** **Exercise**

A Choose the right ones.

1 A: (Whose / Which) shoes are these?

B: These are (their / them) shoes.

2 A: (Whose / Which) toy is this?

B: This is (my brother / my brother's) toy.

3 I have a new computer. My brother has an old computer.

A: (Whose / Which) one is your computer?

B: The new one is (my / his) computer.

4 Eric and Bill have comic books. I have many English books.

A: (Whose / Which) ones are their books?

B: The comic books are (Eric and Bill / Eric and Bill's) books.

B Fill in the blanks.

1 Whose backpack is this? **(Tom)**

⋯▸ This is _____ backpack.

2 Whose car is this? **(parents)**

⋯▸ This is my _____ car.

3 Whose car is red? **(you)**

⋯▸ _____ car is red.

4 Whose bike is this? **(I)**

⋯▸ This is _____ bike.

5 Whose desks are new? **(sisters)**

⋯▸ My _____ desks are new.

6 Whose glasses are these? **(grandfather)**

⋯▸ These are my _____ glasses.

C Make questions and answer them.

1 She has a ribbon.

   Q: __Whose__ __ribbon__ is this?

   A: This is __her__ ribbon.

2 He has a radio.

   Q: _____ _____ is this?

   A: This is _____ radio.

3 They have a black camera.

   Q: _____ one is their camera?

   A: The black _____ is their camera.

4 I have a red umbrella.

   Q: _____ _____ is your umbrella?

   A: The red one is _____ umbrella.

D Fill in the blanks.

1 A: Whose nose is this?

   B: This is the _____ nose.

2 A: Whose horns are these?

   B: These are the _____ horns.

3 A: Whose tail is this?

   B: This is the _____ tail.

4 A: Whose feet are these?

   B: These are the _____ feet.

Word Bank goat   gorilla   squirrel   deer

97

Review Test

A Choose the right ones.

1. I like my dog.
   My dog likes (I / me), too.

2. She likes my brother.
   My brother likes (she / her), too.

3. The cat likes me.
   I like (it / them), too.

4. You know my sister.
   My sister knows (you / your), too.

5. She likes her cousins.
   Her cousins like (she / her), too.

6. We visit our friends on weekends.
   They visit (we / us), too.

7. My brothers need my parents.
   My parents need (they / them), too.

8. He calls his girlfriend every day.
   His girlfriend calls (him / he), too.

B Choose the right ones.

1.

   A: Where is the library?
   B: There is a policeman.
      Ask (he / him / his).

2.

   This is my grandfather.
   I love my grandfather.
   I kiss (his / him / he) every morning.

3.

   She is Jean.
   This is her gift.
   She likes (them / it / they).

4.

   These shoes are dirty!
   Clean (it / they / their / them).

C Fill in the blanks.

1 A: _____ shoes are these?

   B: These are their shoes.

2 A: _____ one is your hat?

   B: The white _____ is my hat.

3 A: _____ bag is that?

   B: That is Emily's bag.

4 A: _____ ones are her hairpins?

   B: The new _____ are her hairpins.

D Fill in the blanks.

1 Mr. Thomas cleans Jason and Tim's room.

   ⋯▸ _____ He _____ cleans _____ their _____ room.

2 Alex feeds the cats.

   ⋯▸ _____ feeds _____.

3 Tina washes her dog every day.

   ⋯▸ _____ washes _____ every day.

4 Mrs. Thomas calls me every day.

   ⋯▸ _____ calls me every day.

5 She and I love our children.

   ⋯▸ _____ love _____.

Challenge Test

A ▸ **Fill in the blanks with pronouns.**

1 Betty likes me and you. ⋯▸ She likes _____.

2 Steve helps you and her. ⋯▸ He helps _____.

3 Ben and Jack like Jim's pets. ⋯▸ _____ like _____ pets.

4 He and I are your best friends. ⋯▸ _____ are your best friends.

5 She and he help Mr. Lee. ⋯▸ They help _____.

6 David knows Mr. Kim and Mrs. Kim. ⋯▸ _____ knows _____.

B ▸ **Correct the wrong ones.**

1 Can ~~your~~ help me?   you

2 This is me new DVD.

3 Her cat likes she.

4 Whose cars are them?

5 This is he MP3 player.

6 This is the children room.

7 Whose pen is this? This is Toms pen.

8 I have a picture. Do you like them?

C ▸ Fill in the blanks to make questions and answers.

1   We have comic books.

Question   _____ comic books are these?

Answer   These are _____ comic books.

2   He has a scooter.

Question   _____ _____ is this?

Answer   This is _____ scooter.

3   They have computers.

Question   _____ _____ are these?

Answer   These are _____ computers.

D ▸ Correct the underlined ones.

Jason: Whose books are these?

Emily: <u>It is</u> my brother's books.
These are
He studies art.

Jason: Look at the toys.

<u>Which</u> toys are these?

Emily: These are my <u>cousin</u> toys.

Jason: Are those your bicycles?

Emily: No. Those are not <u>his</u> bicycles.

Those are <u>my sister and brother</u> bicycles.

Jason: Oh, there is a picture! Look at your family.

<u>Whose</u> one is you?

Emily: The baby in my mom's arms!

Chapter 6

1. Countable noun (easy to count)

	Noun	Singular	Plural
Consonant	**b**ook	a book	two books, three books...
	cat	a cat	two cats, three cats...
	friend	a friend	two friends, three friends...
Vowel (a, e, i, o, u)	**e**gg	an egg	two eggs, three eggs...
	orange	an orange	two oranges, three oranges...
	umbrella	an umbrella	two umbrellas, three umbrellas...

2. Uncountable noun (hard to count)

apple (countable)

water (uncountable)

sand (uncountable)

Countable or uncountable?

1. book _____.   2. milk _____.

Lesson 1

An Apple / Some Milk

 Catch the grammar

Read and fill in the blanks.

A How many apples are there?

⋯▸ **There is** an apple in the basket.

There are six apples in the box.

There are some apples in the box.

an apple

six apples
(= some apples)

B How many coins are there?

⋯▸ **There is** a coin in the jar.

There are _____ coins on the floor.

There are some coins on the floor.

a coin

nine coins
(= some coins)

C How many books are there?

⋯▸ **There is** a book in the bag.

There are _____ books on the shelf.

There are some books on the shelf.

eight books
(= some books)

a book

 Make it yours

1. Countable Noun (easy to count)

First Letter	Singular (There is ~)	Plural (There are ~)	
consonant	a girl	two girls, three girls, four girls…	some girls
vowel	an apple	two apples, three apples, four apples…	some apples

Grammar Point Countable/Uncountable Nouns

1. **Countable noun:** an apple – apples – some apples

2. **Uncountable noun:** water – some water
   (**Some:** for unspecific numbers or quantity)

D **There is some** water in the glass.

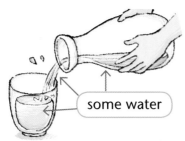

some water

E **There is some** sand in the hole.

some sand

F **There is some** butter on the bread.

some butter

G **There is some** money in the piggy bank.

some money

2. Uncountable Noun (hard to count)

	Some + Noun (There is ~)
No certain form	some water, some milk, some cheese, some butter, some bread
Too small to count	some sand, some salt, some sugar
A group of things	some money, some food

* No singular (a/an), no plural (-s): a water (X), waters (X)

3 Exercise

A Find the countable nouns and the uncountable nouns and fill in the chart.

Countable Nouns			Uncountable Nouns	
_____	_____	_____	_____	_____
_____	_____	_____	_____	_____
_____	_____	_____	_____	_____

B Choose the right ones.

1 (a / an / some) milk in the glass

2 (a / an / some) juice in the cup

3 (a / an / some) money in the purse

4 (a / an / some) apples in the basket

5 (a / an / some) orange in the basket

6 (a / an / some) bananas in the box

C **Choose the right ones.**

1 There (is / are) a pumpkin on the grass.

2 There (is / are) some sugar in the jar.

3 There (is / are) a cake on the table.

4 There (is / are) elephants in the zoo.

5 There (is / are) some coffee in the cup.

6 There (is / are) some water in the jar.

D **Fill in the blanks.**

1

There is _____ orange.

2

There are _____ _____.

3

There is _____ soup in the bowl.

4

There _____ _____ juice in the cup.

5

There _____ _____ pencil on the desk.

6

There _____ _____ _____ on the desk.

107

Many / Much

⭐ Catch the grammar

Look and speak.

A | many = a lot of |

There are **many** cherries.

There are **many** oranges.

There are **many** kiwis.

= There are **a lot of** fruits.

B | a few |

There are **a few** cherries.

There are **a few** oranges.

There are **a few** kiwis.

C | no |

There are **no** cucumbers on the blue dish.

There are **no** pumpkins on the yellow dish.

There are **no** onions on the green dish.

⭐ Make it yours

1. Count Noun: Many, A few, No

There are + many / a few / no + Count Noun (plural)
There are many apples. = There are a lot of apples.
There are a few apples.
There are no apples.

D much = a lot of

There is **much** milk in the glass.

There is **much** juice in the cup.

There is **much** water in the bottle.

= There is **a lot of** water.

E a little

There is **a little** milk in the glass.

There is **a little** juice in the cup.

There is **a little** water in the bottle.

F no

There is **no** milk in the glass.

There is **no** juice in the cup.

There is **no** water in the bottle.

2. Non-count Noun: Much, A little, No

There is + much / a little / no + Non-count Noun (singular)
There is much milk. = There is a lot of milk.
There is a little water.
There is no juice.

109

Exercise

A **Choose the right ones.**

1   There are   (many / a few)   bees on
    the yellow flower.

2   There is   (much / a little)   oil in the
    big bottle.

3   There   (are many / is much)
    strawberry juice in the glass.

    There   (are a few / is a little)   grape
    juice in the glass.

4   There   (is much / are many)   birds
    on the wire.

    There   (is a little / are a few)   birds
    on the branch.

B **Choose the right ones.**

1   There are a few (coins /coin) in the jar.

2   There are many (coin / coins) in the jar.

3   There (is / are) a little water in the bottle.

4   There are a few (pencil / pencils) in the bag.

5   There are many (watermelons / watermelon) at the market.

6   There (is / are) much milk in the cup.

7   There (is / are) many stars in the sky.

C **Fill in the blanks.**

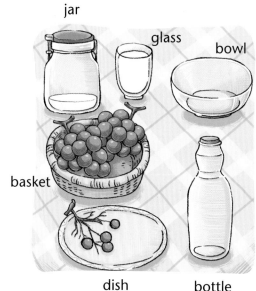

jar

glass

bowl

basket

dish

bottle

1 There is _____ milk in the bottle.

2 There is _____ _____ milk in the jar.

3 There is _____ milk in the glass.

    (= _____ _____ _____)

4 There are _____ grapes in the basket.

5 There are _____ _____ grapes on the dish.

6 There are _____ grapes in the bowl.

| Word Bank | a lot of   much   no   a little   many   a few |

D **Fill in the blanks.**

1 Are there a lot of birds on the alligator? — No. There are ____ _____ birds.

2 Are there a lot of birds in the tree? — Yes. There are _____ birds.

3 Are there many birds on the road? — No. There are _____ birds.

4 Is there much water in the pond? — No. There _____ _____ water.

| Word Bank | many   a few   no |

Some / Any

⭐ Catch the grammar

Read and check the right answers.

Ⓐ Oh, I need an eraser.

Do you have **any** erasers?

- ☐ **Yes**, I have **some** erasers in my pencil case.
- ☑ **No**, I don't have **any** erasers in my pencil case.

Ⓑ Oh, there are things for animals!

Does he have **any** animals?

- ☐ **Yes**, he has **some** animals.
- ☐ **No**, he doesn't have **any** animals.

⭐ Make it yours

1. Some / Any (for countable)

	Some (affirmative) / Any (question and negative)
Affirmative	There are some books on the shelf.
Question	Are there any books on the shelf?
Answer	Yes, there are some books.
	No, there are not any books.

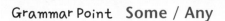

> **Grammar Point   Some / Any**
>
> 1. **Some**: for affirmatives
> 2. **Any**: for questions and negatives

C I'm thirsty!

Is there **any** water in the bottle?

- ☐ **Yes**, there is **some** water in the bottle.
- ☐ **No**, there is not **any** water in the bottle.

- -

D Does Judy have **any** juice?

- ☐ **Yes**, she has **some** juice.
- ☐ **No**, she doesn't have **any** juice.

Do Tom and Jane have **any** milk?

- ☐ **Yes**, they have **some** milk.
- ☐ **No**, they do not have **any** milk.

Judy   Jane   Tom

2. Some / Any (for uncountable)

	Some (affirmative) / Any (question and negative)
Affirmative	There is some milk in the bottle.
Question	Is there any milk in the bottle?
Answer	Yes, there is somme milk.
	No, there is not any milk.

⭐ Exercise

A Choose the right ones.

1 Are there (some / any) seals?

→ Yes, there are (some / any) seals.

2 Are there (some / any) cats?

→ No, there are not (some / any) cats.
There are (some / any) dogs.

3 Is there (some / any) water?

→ Yes, there is (some / any) water.

B Fill in the blanks.

1 A: Do you have _____ money?

B: No, I do not have _____ money.

2 A: Does the brown dog have _____ bones?

B: Yes, it has _____ bones.

3 A: Does your grandfather have _____ hair?

B: No, he does not have _____ hair.

4 A: Does the girl have _____ cookies?

B: Yes, she has _____ cookies.

C Correct the wrong ones.

1 No, there is not some water in the can.   _____any_____

2 There are any books.   _____

3 There are some milk.   _____

4 There is not some juice in the glass.   _____

5 No, he doesn't have some tea.   _____

6 Are there any butter now?   _____

D Fill in the blanks.

1 A: I am thirsty. Is there ___any___ juice in the jar?

   B: _____, there is not _____ juice in the jar.

   A: _____ there _____ chocolate milk in the cup?

   B: _____, there is _____ chocolate milk in the cup.

2 A: I am hungry. _____ there _____ soup in the bowl?

   B: _____, there _____ _____ soup in the bowl.

3 A: I want some books. _____ there _____ books on the table?

   B: Yes, there _____ _____ books on the table.

Review Test

A Choose the right ones.

1 There is (a / an / some) peanut in the jar.

2 There are (a / an / some) peanuts in the basket.

3 There is (a / an / some) butter on the bread.

4 There (is / are) a little butter in the can.

5 There (is / are) many pencils in the drawer.

6 There (is / are) a little sand in the truck.

7 There (are / is) a few children in the playground.

8 There are (many / much) dolphins in the sea.

9 There is (a few / a little) water in the pond.

B Circle all the right words for the blanks.

There is a + _____	school, desk, books, butter, water, apples, orange, eagle, sand, elephant, pencil

There is an + _____	school, desk, books, butter, water, apples, orange, eagle, sand, elephant, pencil

There is some + _____	school, desk, books, butter, water, apples, orange, eagle, sand, elephant, pencil

There are some + _____	school, desk, books, butter, water, apples, oranges, eagles, sand, elephants, pencil

C) Write the opposites.

1   There are many melons.   ⟷   There are _____ _____ melons.

2   There is much water in the jar.   ⟷   There is _____ _____ water in the jar.

D) Fill in the blanks.

1   A: I need some cookies.

     Are there _____ cookies on the dish?

    B: Yes, there _____ _____ cookies.

2   A: She is thirsty.

     Do you have _____ water?

    B: No, I don't _____ _____ _____.

3   A: Are there any people in the restaurant?

    B: _____, there _____ _____ _____ people
    in the restaurant.

E) Unscramble.

1   is / there / water / a lot of / in the jar   _____.

2   are / there / some / candies   _____.

3   have / I / a / few / books / in my room   _____.

4   a / little / she / ice cream / has   _____.

Challenge Test

A▸ Fill in the blanks.

1   There are _____ cherries in the bowl.

2   There are _____ cherries in the glass.

3   There are _____ cherries on the dish.

4   There is _____ water in the cup.

5   There is _____ juice in the glass.

6   There is _____ milk in the jar.

> **Word Bank**   no   a lot of   a few   a little

B▸ Answer the questions.

> I need to buy some fruits today.

1   Do you have ___any___ melons?   ⋯▸ __Yes__ , _I have some melons_ .

2   Do you have _____ oranges?   ⋯▸ _____ , _____ .

3   Do you have _____ grapes?   ⋯▸ _____ , _____ .

4   Do you have _____ apples?   ⋯▸ _____ , _____ .

C Correct the wrong ones.

1 There is̶ many toys.
are

2 There is some notebooks.

3 There is any milk.

4 There is many juice in the glass.

5 There are not some books in the drawer.

6 There is any ice cream in the refrigerator.

D Fill in the blanks.

1 There ___is___ ___some___ orange juice in the glass.

2 There _____ _____ orange juice in the bottle.

3 There _____ ____ _____ apples on the table.

4 There _____ _____ apples in the basket.

5 There _____ ____ _____ water in the cup.

6 There _____ _____ soup in the bowl.

7 There _____ _____ books on the table.

8 There _____ ____ _____ ____ forks on the dish.

9 There _____ _____ steaks on the dish.

10 There _____ _____ spoons on the table.

Word Bank

much

a few

a little

no

some

a lot of

MeMo

First Step in Grammar

Workbook

2

Clue & Key

First Step in Grammar

2

Workbook

Clue & Key

Chapter 1   Lesson 1

 Review the grammar points.

Circle the subjects (who) and underline the be-verbs.

(I) am happy.	You are happy.
He is angry.	They are angry.
She is sad.	We are sad.

Circle the subjects (who) and underline the common verbs.

She goes to the gym every day.
I wash my hands every day.
They study at night every day.

A. **Find the subjects (who and what) and match the right ones.**

1. Who is in the boat? •   • The sailor is in the boat.

2. Who is in the plane? •   • The crocodile is on the land.

3. What is on the land? •   • The dolphin is in the sea.

4. What is on the rock? •   • The pilot is in the plane.

5. What is in the sea? •   • The turtle is on the rock.

B. Find the subjects (who) and underline them.

1. John is on his bike.

2. Tim and Greta are on a boat.

3. Janice is sad. She is sick today.

4. They are at a party.

5. He is in his math classroom.

C. Circle the be-verbs and underline the common verbs.

1. She is a dancer.
   She dances after school every day.

2. I am an artist.
   I paint in my art class every day.

3. My sister is friendly.
   She helps many people.

4. I am very smart.
   I read many books.

5. My sister is tall.
   She plays basketball.

6. Jim is a good doctor.
   He works at a hospital.

7. Ginger and I are teachers.
   We help our students.

Review the grammar points.

Fill in the blanks.

I	read	a newspaper	every morning.
You	write	an email	every day.
They	run	far	every Saturday.
We	eat	early	every night.
He	( )	a newspaper every morning.	
She	( )	an email every Saturday.	
It	( )	far every day.	
	( )	early every night.	

A. Choose the right ones.

1 It is a robot.
   It (moves / move) the box.

2 You are good soccer players.
   You (play / plays) soccer well.

3 I eat cookies every day.
   They (eat / eats) cookies every day.

4 She (reads / read) the news every day.
   I (reads / read) emails every day.

5 My neighbors are at the market.
   They (buy / buys) food every day.
   He (buy / buys) food every day, too.

6 We are good runners.
   We (run / runs) races every day.
   My dog (run / runs) races every day, too.

7 Terry (throw / throws) a ball well.
   I (throw / throws) a ball well, too.

8 My cats (like / likes) the toy.
   My dog (hate / hates) the cats.

B. Fill in the blanks.

1. There ____are____ many classes in my school. **(be)**

2. Barbara _____ my cousin. **(be)**

3. She _____ a song in music class. **(sing)**

4. Tim _____ a fun story in writing class. **(write)**

5. Jenny _____ many pictures in an art class. **(draw)**

6. We _____ English books every day. **(read)**

7. My brother _____ a good student. **(be)**

8. He _____ many students with their homework. **(help)**

9. He _____ busy every day. **(be)**

10. My brother and I _____ computer games every day. **(play)**

11. Jenny _____ a bus every day. **(ride)**

C. Correct the underlined ones.

1. She <u>study</u> in class.   studies

2. You <u>studies</u> at home.

3. He <u>read</u> the newspaper every day.

4. I <u>jumps</u> rope with them.

5. We <u>runs</u> fast on the playground.

6. It <u>eat</u> many worms.

5

Chapter 1   Lesson 3

 Review the grammar points.

Fill in the blanks.

I, You, We, They	read	write	drink	eat
He, She, It	reads	( )	( )	( )

I, You, We, They	study	wash	watch	do
He, She, It	studies	( )	( )	( )

A. Choose the right ones.

1. Bill fries / fry potatoes well.
   I fries / fry potatoes well.

2. They are good students.
   They study / studies every day.

3. You watch / watches TV every day. Mr. Lee watch / watches TV every day.

4. I drinks / drink juice every day.
   He drinks / drink milk every day.

5. Nancy goes / go to the gym every day.
   They goes / go to the pool every day.

6. We does / do puzzles every weekend.
   He does / do exercises every weekend.

7. I teach / teaches my class every day.
   She teach / teaches her class every day.

8. Dad wash / washes the car every day.
   They wash / washes the car every day.

B. Fill in the blanks.

1 They wash their hands every day.

The boy _____ his hand every day, too.

2 The baby pigs say, "Oink! Oink!"

The kitten _____ , "Meow! Meow!"

3 I go to church every Sunday.

Linda _____ to the movie every Sunday.

4 My brothers watch TV every day.

My dad _____ TV every day.

5 The bugs fly at night.
The bird _____ high in the sky.

C. Fill in the blanks.

1 every _____

2 every _____

3 every _____

4 on _____

| Saturday, Sunday |
| Mon., Tue., Wed., Thu., Fri., Sat., Sun. |
| Jan., Feb., Mar., Apr. ... December |
| 2010, 2011, 2012, 2013... |

D. Correct the underlined ones.

1 They <u>goes</u> to church on Sundays.

2 She <u>dry</u> the towels in the sun.

3 I <u>goes</u> to the mall every weekend.

7

Review the grammar points.

Fill in the blanks.

I, They, We, You	
Affirmative	I **like** ice cream.
Negative	I ( ) ( ) **like** ice cream.
Contraction	I ( ) **like** ice cream.
She, He, It	
Affirmative	She **likes** donuts.
Negative	She ( ) ( ) **like** donuts.
Contraction	She ( ) **like** donuts.

A. Choose the right ones.

1. This is a frog. It (do not / does not) eat fish.

2. This is Mrs. Kim. She (do not / does not) live in the apartment.

3. They (do not / does not) watch old movies.

4. Cindy plays badminton, but she does not (play / plays) basketball.

5. Jim studies on school days, but he does not (study / studies) on weekends.

B. Fill in the blanks.

1. My sister _____ milk, but she does not _____ coffee. **(drink)**

2. They _____ on warm days, but they do not _____ on cold days. **(run)**

3. She _____ in the swimming pool every day, but he does not _____ on Sundays. **(swim)**

4. He _____ not visit his grandmother every day, but his sister _____. **(do)**

C. Make negatives.

1. He likes pizza. _____

2. I ride the train every day. _____

3. She eats cereal every morning. _____

4. They sing every day. _____

5. She cooks pizza every Saturday. _____

6. It likes the little girl. _____

7. We ride bikes every morning. _____

8. You drink milk every night. _____

D. Correct the underlined ones.

1. They <u>does not like</u> the music.

2. She <u>does not answers</u> the phone.

3. I <u>do not learns</u> songs well.

4. It <u>do not jump</u> on the bed.

5. He <u>doesn't likes</u> the cats.

6. We <u>dont go</u> to the gym.

7. They <u>doesn't ski</u> on the mountain.

8. Judy <u>doesn't eats</u> in bed.

Chapter 2   Lesson 1

 Review the grammar points.

Fill in the blanks.

I, We, You, They	
Affirmative	I **live** in an apartment.
Question	( ) you ( ) in an apartment?
Answer	Yes, I ( ). (= Yes, I live in an apartment.)
	No, I don't. (= No, I ( ) ( ) ( ) in an apartment.)

She, He, It	
Affirmative	She **lives** in an apartment.
Question	( ) she ( ) in an apartment?
Answer	Yes, she ( ). (= Yes, she lives in an apartment.)
	No, she doesn't. (= No, she ( ) ( ) ( ) in an apartment.)

A. **Choose the right ones.**

1 (Does / Do) he like the girl?
➡ Yes, he (does / do).

2 (Does / Do) you listen to the radio?
➡ No, I (doesn't / don't).

3 Do you (take / takes) the bus every morning?
➡ No, I (don't / doesn't).

4 Does the mouse (cry / cries), "Meow! Meow!"
➡ No, it (don't / doesn't).

5 (Does / Do) Tom like Chinese food?
➡ No, he (doesn't / don't).

6 Do they (swim / swims) every day?
➡ Yes, they (do / does).

7 (Does / Do) Bill like the sandwich?
➡ No, he (doesn't / don't).

8 Do the cats (play / plays) with the toy all day?
➡ Yes, they (do / does).

B. Make questions and answers.

	Affirmative	Question / Answer
1	She sleeps in the bed.	Q: _____ she _____ in the bed? A: Yes, _____ _____.
2	Mr. James goes to the park every Sunday.	Q: _____ he _____ to the park every Sunday? A: No, _____ _____.
3	They play soccer in the afternoon.	Q: _____ they _____ soccer in the afternoon? A: Yes, _____ _____.
4	I sail on a ship.	Q: _____ you _____ on a ship? A: Yes, I _____.
5	Judy likes the cakes.	Q: _____ she _____ the cakes? A: No, she _____.

C. Find the wrong ones and rewrite.

1. Do you brushes the dog every day?   Do you brush the dog every day?

2. Do he give money to you?   _____

3. They don't dances at the concert.   _____

4. We do not likes the cake.   _____

5. She doesn't eats fish.   _____

6. Yes, I likes strawberries.   _____

7. No, we does not stay in the room.   _____

8. It don't move fast in the evening.   _____

11

Review the grammar points.

Fill in the blanks.

You are a good student.				
Question	(			)
Answer	Yes, (	).	No, (	).

He is a good student.				
Question	(			)
Answer	Yes, (	).	No, (	).

You like the dog.				
Question	(			)
Answer	Yes, (	).	No, (	).
Wh-question	What (	) you like?		

He likes the dog.				
Question	(			)
Answer	Yes, (	).	No, (	).
Wh-question	What (	) he like?		

A. **Choose the right ones.**

1. (Is / Are / Does) she a good friend? ➡ Yes, she (is / is not / does / does not).

2. (Am / Are / Do) you a painter? ➡ No, I (am / am not / does / does not).

3. (Is / Am / Does / Do) it a puppy? ➡ No, it (isn't / am not / does not).

4. (Does / Do / Are) you like fish? ➡ No, I (do not / does not / am not).

5. (Does / Do / Are) they like winter? ➡ No, they (doesn't / don't / are not).

6. Do the boys (kick / kicks) the soccer balls every day? ➡ Yes, they (do / does).

7. What does he (do / does)? ➡ He (teach / teaches) English.

8. Does the cat (eat / eats) the cheese? ➡ No, it (don't / doesn't).

B. Fill in the blanks.

1 A: Are they in the swimming pool?

B: _____, they _____ in the swimming pool.

2 A: What does Grace like?

B: She _____ _____.

3 A: Is he at home?

B: _____, he _____ _____ at home.

4 A: Does it like milk?

B: Yes, it _____.

milk

5 A: Are you hungry?

B: _____, I_____ _____ hungry.

C. Correct the underlined ones.

1 <u>Are you like</u> the puzzle?

2 What <u>do she like</u>?

3 <u>Do you</u> a nurse?

4 They <u>is firemen</u> in our city.

5 No, <u>I are not</u> at school on Saturdays.

6 <u>Do it catch</u> fish in the winter?

7 What <u>does rabbits eat</u>?

8 <u>Does you eat</u> chocolate candy at lunch?

Chapter 2　Lesson 3

 Review the grammar points.

Fill in the blanks.

| I /You /We /They / Boys　+ **have** + dogs. |
| He / She / It　　　　　　 + **has**　+ dogs. |

I have a new game CD.	(　　　) you (　　　) a new game CD?
	Yes, I (　　　　). / No I (　　　　　).
She has a new game CD.	(　　　) she (　　　) a new game CD?
	Yes, she (　　　). / No, she (　　　　).

A. Choose the right ones.

1　The ant　have / has　a small body.
But the beetle　have / has　a
large body.

2　We　have / has　rice every day.
But Mr. Smith doesn't　have / has
rice every day.

3　My dad　have / has　brown eyes.
I　have / has　brown eyes, too.

4　Do you　have / has　a question?
Yes, I do. I　have / has　a question.

5　Does Kevin　have / has　noodles
at lunch?
Yes, he　have / has　noodles at
lunch.

6　The students　have / has　six
classes every day.
They don't　have / has　gym class
every day.

7　What does she　have / has　in the
box?
She　have / has　a gift in the box.

8　Does it　have / has　a long tail?
No, it doesn't　have / has　a long
tail.

9　The boy　have / has　boots.
But he does not　have / has　an
umbrella.

10　The dog　have / has　brown fur.
But it　don't / doesn't　have brown
eyes.

Fill in the blanks.

1. A: What does she have in the basket?

   B: _____ _____ eggs in the basket.

   ①

2. A: My brother has long legs.

   B: But I _____ short _____.

   ②

3. A: Do you have a pen?

   B: _____, I _____ _____ a pen.

   ③

4. A: Does Frank have rollerblades?

   B: _____, he _____ rollerblades under the desk.

   ④

   ⑤

5. A: The black dog has a bone.

   B: But the white dog _____ _____ a bone.

C. **Find the wrong ones and rewrite.**

1. They don't has many flowers. _____

2. We has a vase in the living room. _____

3. What do she have in the bag? _____

4. Does you have a cold? _____

5. You has a pretty room. _____

6. He doesn't has a hat. _____

7. Does Emily has a class at 2:00? _____

Review the grammar points.

Fill in the blanks.

I am **happy**.	I smile **happily**.
He is a **bad** player.	He plays ( ).
He is a **slow** runner.	He runs ( ).
He is a **quiet** boy.	He talks ( ).
The plane is **fast**.	It flies ( ).
He is **late**.	He comes ( ).
He is a **hard** worker.	He works ( ).
He is a **good** painter.	He paints ( ).

A. **Choose the right ones.**

1 He plays his guitar (quiet / quietly).
He is a (quiet / quietly) player.

2 The wolf is (angry / angrily).
It hollows (angry / angrily).

3 She is (happy / happily).
She laughs (happy / happily).

4 She is a (sad / sadly) girl.
She cries (sad / sadly).

5 She is a (good / well) tennis player.
She plays (good / well).

6 He is a (bad / badly) pianist.
He plays the piano (bad / badly).

7 They are (slow / slowly) workers.
They work (slow / slowly).

8 They shout (noisy / noisily).
They are (noisy / noisily).

9 The bus is (late / lately).
The bus comes (late / lately) every evening.

10 They dance (beautiful / beautifully).
They are (beautiful / beautifully) dancers.

B. Fill in the blanks.

1. Tom is a fast runner.
   He runs _____ .

2. He is late for school every day.
   He goes to school _____ every day.

3. My sister is a good cook.
   She cooks _____ .

4. Tom is a slow runner.
   He runs _____ .

5. Jane is a beautiful singer.
   She sings _____ .

6. Emily is happy.
   She smiles _____ .

C. Choose the right verbs.

1.
I	am	happy.
	smile	

2.
I	am	happily.
	smile	

3.
She	is	beautiful.
	dances	

4.
She	is	beautifully.
	dances	

D. Correct the underlined ones.

1. My brother cooks <u>good</u>.

2. I play sports <u>poor</u>, but my brother plays well.

3. My brother talks to me <u>kind</u> and does not speak angrily.

4. He sings <u>beautiful</u> to me at bedtime.

5. He is <u>quietly</u>.

6. I love my <u>wonderfully</u> brother.

17

Review the grammar points.

Fill in the blanks.

She can run fast.		
Negative	She (	) run fast.
Contraction	She (	) run fast.
Question	( ) she (	) fast?
Answer	Yes, she (	). / No, she ( ).

A. **Read and answer the questions.**

The turtle can crawl.
The turtle cannot hop.
The turtle can swim in the water.
The turtle cannot eat carrots.

The rabbit cannot crawl.
The rabbit can hop.
The rabbit cannot swim in the water.
The rabbit can eat carrots.

1 Can the rabbit hop? _____ , it _____.

2 Can the turtle crawl? _____ , it _____.

3 Can the rabbit swim in the water? _____ , it _____.

4 Can the rabbit crawl? _____ , it _____.

5 Can the rabbit eat carrots? _____ , it _____.

6 Can the turtle hop? _____ , it _____.

7 Can the turtle swim in the water? _____ , it _____.

B. Fill in the blanks.

1. A fish _____ swim well, but a rabbit _____ swim well.

2. A kangaroo _____ jump high, but the turtle _____ jump high.

3. My brother is slow. He _____ run fast.

4. Judy: Hello! Can I talk to Bobby now?

   Mom: Bobby is sick, so you _____ talk to him now.

5. You _____ eat in the kitchen. You cannot eat in the classroom.

6. The dog _____ chase the cat well.

7. My sister has a cold. She _____ swim now.

8. My brother is sick. So, he _____ study now.

C. Correct the underlined ones.

1. Karen <u>can sings</u> beautifully.
   > can sing

2. Bob <u>can watches</u> TV now.

3. Jim <u>wins can</u> a race every weekend.

4. A hen <u>can not fly</u>.

5. We <u>cann't play</u> baseball now.

6. A: Can George go to school now?

   B: <u>Yes, he cannot</u>. He is sick.

7. A: Can you run fast?

   B: Yes, I <u>cannot</u>!

Review the grammar points.

Fill in the blanks.

You must go now.			
Negative	You (	) (	) (	) now.

You should sleep now.			
Negative	You (	) (	) (	) now.
Question	(	) I (	) now?	
Answer	Yes, you (	). / No, you (	) (	).

A. Choose the right ones.

1　Don't talk. Be quiet!
   You　must not / must　talk here.

2　Your shoes are wet.
   You　should not / do not　wear them.

3　You are sick.
   You　do / should　see a doctor.

4　A: Should / Do　I eat this?
   B: Yes, you　should / do .

5　A: Should I sleep now?
   B: Yes, you　should / do .

6　Watch out!
   You　must wait / wait　here.

7　Be careful! You　must not / do not　cross the street now.

8　The dentist says, "You　should / can　brush your teeth every day."

9　Oh, these are dirty clothes. You　do not / should not　wear them.

10　You play soccer well. You　should / should not　play in the soccer team.

B. Unscramble.

1. should / I / the guitar / play _____.

2. must / he / not / on the floor / sleep _____.

3. sing / in the room / must / you / not _____.

4. sleep / should / you / now _____.

5. run / you / not / should _____.

C. Make negatives.

1. Oh, the water is dirty! <u>You should drink the water.</u>

   ➡ _____

2. The chair is wet. <u>You should sit on the chair.</u>

   ➡ _____

3. We have a red light. <u>We must go across the street.</u>

   ➡ _____

D. Correct the underlined ones.

1. You <u>not must</u> cross the street here!

2. You <u>must not walks</u> in the tall grass.

3. He <u>should studies</u> now.

4. You <u>not should</u> eat that candy.

5. She <u>should is</u> quiet.

Review the grammar points.

Fill in the blanks.

Question	Answer
( ) do you eat for a snack?	I eat cookies.
( ) do you like?	I like Jane.
( ) cookies do you eat?	I eat chocolate cookies.
( ) one do you need, A or B?	I need A and B. = I need ( ).

A. **Choose the right ones.**

1   A: Is this chocolate ice cream?
    B: No, it isn't.
    A: (What / Which) is it?
    B: It's vanilla ice cream.

2   A: Do you like Jason?
    B: No, I don't like him.
    A: (Who / What) do you like?
    B: I like my teacher. She is very nice.

3   A: It is rainy today.
    B: (What / Who) do you need?
    A: I need a raincoat.
    B: (Who / Which) raincoat do you need, the long raincoat or the short raincoat?

B. **Unscramble.**

1   what / eat / do / you / for breakfast _____?

2   does / which / she / like / juice _____?

3   like / does / Judy / who _____?

4   she / like / does / apples / which / fruit / or / grapes

_____?

C. Fill in the blanks.

1 _____ animal do you like, the hamster or the parrot?

2 A: _____ vegetable do you want for lunch, the carrots or the beans?
B: I want the beans.

3 A: _____ do you like?
B: I like Susan.

4 A: _____ pizza do you want, the pepperoni or the cheese pizza?
B: I want both.

5 Susan likes Jason. _____ do you like?

6 _____ brushes do you like, the long or the short ones?

7 _____ boy does my sister like, Jason or Ben?

D. Correct the underlined ones.

1 <u>What</u> do you like? — I like Ann.

2 <u>Who dog</u> does your brother like, the
white one or the brown one?

3 <u>Who</u> do you like, apples or watermelons?

4 <u>What one</u> does she need, a fork or a spoon?

5 <u>Which</u> are you? — I am Mary Smith.

6 <u>Which</u> is it? — It is a cheese pizza.

7 Is the short girl your sister? — No, she isn't.
— <u>What</u> is she?

Chapter 4 Lesson 2

 Review the grammar points.

Fill in the blanks.

Question	Answer
( ) do you play the piano?	I play every Saturday (= on Saturdays).
( ) do you sleep?	I sleep ( ) night.
( ) do you wake up?	I wake up at 6:00 ( ) the morning.
( ) do you study every day?	I study ( ) my room.
( ) does she go every Sunday?	She goes ( ) church.

A. **Choose the right ones.**

1 Where / When does the bear live? ➡ It lives in / on the woods.

2 Where / When does Joseph go every Friday? ➡ He goes to the movies.

3 Where / When can you play with me? ➡ We can play in / on the afternoon.

4 Where / When does George have art class? ➡ He has art class on / at
                                                                    Tuesdays.

5 Where / When do they go to sleep? ➡ They go to sleep at / on 9:00.

6 When do you wake up in / on the morning? ➡ I wake up at / on 7:00.

7 Where / When does she go every Monday? ➡ She goes to / at the library.

8 Where / When do you play? ➡ I play on the playground.

B. Fill in the blanks.

1. _____ do you go to school? — I go to school at Westbury Middle School.

2. _____ is the new theater? — It is on Broad Street across from the bank.

3. _____ do you see you friends? — I see my friends on Sunday afternoons.

4. _____ do you eat lunch? — I eat lunch at 1:00 p.m.

5. _____ is the English book? — It is next to the math book.

6. _____ does she have dance class? — She has it on Thursday afternoon.

C. Fill in the blanks.

1. A: When do you have a piano class?

   B: I have a piano class _____ Thursday.

2. A: Where does he go every summer?

   B: He goes _____ an island.

3. A: When do you do your homework?

   B: I do my homework _____ night.

D. Correct the wrong ones.

1. When does he study math? — He studies it at school.

   Where

2. Where do you swim? — I swim the swimming pool.

3. Where does Jane go in Sundays? — She goes to church.

4. Where are my pencils? — They are at the desk.

5. When does the movie start? — It starts in 4:00 p.m.

25

Review the grammar points.

Fill in the blanks.

Question	Answer
( ) does it look?	It looks (good / house).
( ) does it feel?	It feels (doll / soft).
( ) does it look ( )?	It looks like (a gorilla / bad).

A.   Choose the right ones.

1 How does it feel? ➡ It feels   hard / a hard rock   .

2   How / What   does it taste like? ➡ It tastes like   spicy / a hot pepper   .

3 How does it taste? ➡ It tastes   spicy / a hot pepper   .

4   How / What   does she look like? ➡ She looks like   pretty / a princess   .

5 How does she look? ➡ She looks   pretty / a princess   .

6   How / What   does it smell like? ➡ It smells like a skunk!

7   How / What   does it smell? ➡ It smells bad!

8 What does it taste like? ➡ It tastes   like cheese / cheese   .

9 What does it feel like? ➡ It feels   like a bumpy rock / bump   .

10   How / What   does he look like? ➡ He looks like   nice / his father   .

11 How does it sound? ➡ It sounds   beautiful / a cry   .

12 What does it look like? ➡ It looks   like a circle / a circle   .

B. Fill in the blanks.

1. How does she look? — She _____ smart.

2. What does this feel like? — It _____ _____ a rock.

3. What does it taste like? — It _____ _____ ice cream.

4. What does it smell like? — It _____ _____ a rose.

5. What does it look _____? — It _____ _____ a monkey.

6. Do I look _____ my brother? — No, you don't.

7. _____ does it smell like? — It _____ _____ coffee.

C. Correct the underlined ones.

1. <u>What does it smell?</u> — It smells like popcorn.

2. How does this feel? — <u>It feels like soft.</u>

3. <u>How do they feel like?</u> — They feel angry.

4. <u>What does it look?</u> — It looks like a gorilla.

D. Unscramble.

1. looks / princess / like / she / a   _____.

2. like / coffee / smells / it   _____.

3. taste / food / the / how / does   _____?

Review the grammar points.

Fill in the blanks.

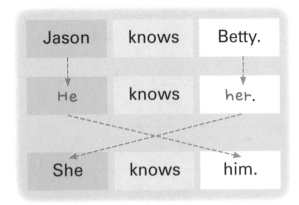

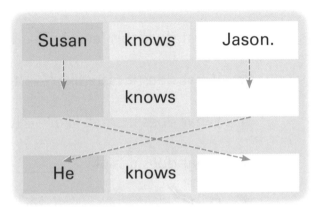

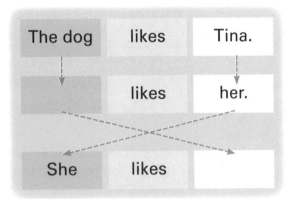

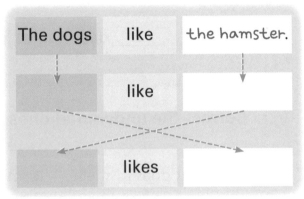

A. Choose the right ones.

1. George knows (I / me). = (He / She) knows (I / me).

2. The cat likes the fish. = (It / They) likes the fish.

3. Jim knows Angela. = (He / Him) knows (she / her).

4. Betty likes the dogs. = (He / She / Him / Her) likes (it / them).

5. Susan likes (us / we). We like (she / her), too.

6. Sheila eats bananas in the morning. She eats (it / them) every morning.

7. Jane helps her friend Tom. (He / She / Him / Her) helps (he / she / him / her), too.

8. Judy and Emily clean the rooms on Tuesdays. (They / Them) clean (it / them) well

B. Fill in the blanks.

1. They clean <u>the desk</u> every day.   = They clean ___it___ every day.

2. Jason and I wash <u>our dogs</u> every day. = _____ wash _____ every day.

3. I like <u>the students</u>.   = I like _____.

4. She helps <u>my dad</u> every day.   = She helps _____ every day.

5. He helps <u>me and him</u> every day.   = He helps _____ every day.

6. They know <u>you and him</u>.   = They know _____.

C. Choose the right ones.

1. Do you like (her / him / them)?

2. Does he like (her / him / them)?

3. Do you know (her / him / them)?

D. Find the wrong ones and rewrite.

1. He likes she.   _____

2. They know I.   _____

3. Me like her.   _____

4. I like he.   _____

5. Her studies English.   _____

6. He helps we every day. _____

Chapter 5   Lesson 2

 Review the grammar points.

Fill in the blanks.

Subject	Possessive	Object
I am Tom.	I like ( ) teacher.	He likes ( ).
You are Betty.	I like ( ) teacher.	I like ( ).
He is John.	I like ( ) bike.	I like ( ).
She is Susan.	I like ( ) sweater.	I like ( ).
It is Rex.	I like ( ) fur.	I like ( ).
We are a family.	They like ( ) house.	They like ( ).
They are my friends.	I like ( ) shoes.	I like ( ).

A. **Choose the right ones.**

1 You like   you / your   cat. The cat likes   you / your , too.

2 He likes   he / his   cat. The cat likes   he / his / him , too.

3 She likes   she / her   cat. The cat likes   she / her , too.

4 They like   they / their   cat. The cat likes   they / their / them , too.

5 I like   my / me   cat. The cat likes   I / my / me , too.

6 We like   we / our   cat. The cat likes   we / our / us , too.

B. **Fill in the blanks.**

I am Kevin. Please, help _____!

My dogs are dirty. Wash _____, please!

Look at _____! She is sick now.

C. Fill in the blanks.

1. You have many animals. Can I draw _____?

2. Is this your book? Can I borrow _____?

3. He is very handsome. Can I draw _____?

4. There is a big box. Can I open _____?

5. We are basketball players. These are _____ shirts.

6. Does he know Judy? — Yes, he knows _____.

D. Fill in the blanks.

Look at the man. _____ is very tall.

I like _____ sweater.

Look at the woman. _____ is very pretty.

I like _____ dogs. _____ are cute.

I like _____.

E. Correct the wrong ones.

1. You are a good musician. Play your guitar, please! Play them, please.
   it

2. She likes his new bike. She rides it every day.

3. This is my son. Please draw her.

4. My grandparents cook rice cakes well. His rice cake is really good.

5. This is we basketball coach. We like him.

6. Sara eats rice cakes on the weekend. It likes them.

7. This is my history teacher. Me like he.

Review the grammar points.

Fill in the blanks.

Question	Answer
Whose books are these?	These are (　　　　) books. (I)
	These are (　　　　) books. (Tom)
	These are (　　　　　) books. (Tom and Susan)
	These are (　　　　　) books. (my brothers)
(　　　　) car is this?	This is (　　　　　) car. (my parents)
(　　　　) one is your room?	The messy one is my room.

A. **Choose the right ones.**

1 (Whose / Which) TV is the new one? — The new one is (his / him) TV.

2 He has many toys on his desk. I have many books on my desk.
　 (Whose / Which) ones are his things? — The toys are (his / my) things.

3 (Whose / Which) pen is this? — This is my (teachers / teacher's) pen.

4 (Whose / Which) one is my parents' car? — The blue one is (her / their) car.

5 (Whose / Which) glasses are these?
　 — These are my (grandmother's / grandmother') glasses.

6 (Whose / Which) one is your book? — The big one is (me / my) book.

B. Fill in the blanks.

① Tim

② Susan

③ students

④ Tom and Bill

⑤ you and Cindy

⑥ brothers

1. Whose socks are those?
   ➡ Those are _____ socks.

2. Whose backpack is that?
   ➡ That is _____ backpack.

3. Whose books are those?
   ➡ Those are the _____
   books.

4. Whose umbrellas are those?
   ➡ Those are _____
   umbrellas.

5. Whose candies are those?
   ➡ Those are _____
   candies!

6. Whose bicycles are these?
   ➡ These are my _____ bicycles.

C. Unscramble.

1. bicycle / is / this / whose
   _____?

2. your / ones / which / are / toys
   _____?

3. whose / are / socks / these
   _____?

Review the grammar points.

Fill in the blanks.

First Letter	Singular	Plural	
Vowel (a, e, i, o, u)	( ) apple	two ( ), three ( ) some ( )	
Consonant	( ) girl	two ( ), three ( ) some ( )	

	Singular	Plural	Some ~
water			( ) water
butter	X	X	( ) butter
milk			( ) milk
sand			( ) sand

A. **Choose the right ones.**

1 There is   a / an / some   juice in the glass.

2 There are   a / an / some   peanuts on the plate.

3 There are   a / an / some   boys on the playground.

4 There is   a / an / some   water in the cup.

5 There   is / are   an apple in the box.

6 There   is / are   some coffee in the cup.

7 There   is / are   some soup in the bowl.

8 There   is / are   a melon in the basket.

9 There   is / are   some melons in the basket.

B. **Fill in the blanks.**

1. A: How many girls _____ _____ in this room?

   B: There _____ _____ girl in this room.

2. _____ _____ some butter on this bread.

3. _____ _____ _____ sandwiches in my lunchbox.

4. _____ _____ some water in the glass.

5. _____ _____ some money in the piggy bank.

6. _____ _____ some grapes on the dish.

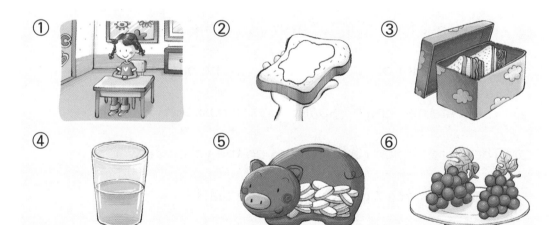

C. **Correct the wrong ones.**

1. There are some butter on the bread. | is

2. There is two bananas in the basket.

3. There are some money in the purse.

4. There is some dogs in the house.

Review the grammar points.

Fill in the blanks.

There (   ) many apples. = There are (a) (lot) (of) apples.

There (   ) a few apples.

There (   ) much milk.   = There is ( ) (   ) (   ) milk.

There (   ) a little juice.

A. **Choose the right ones.**

1   There are many   marble / marbles   in the bag.

2   There are a few   marble / marbles   in the bag.

3   Are there a lot of   apple / apples   in the basket?

4   There are no   apple / apples   in the basket.

5   There are   much / many   bees on the yellow flower.

6   There is   much / many   milk in the glass.

7   There are   a few / a little   flowers in the vase.

8   There is   a few / a little   milk in the glass.

9   There   is / are   much milk in the cup.

10   There   is / are   many apples in the basket.

11   There   is / are   a little juice in the bottle.

12   There   is / are   some pears on the shelf.

B. Fill in the blanks.

1 There _____ many fish.

2 There _____ a little water in the cup.

3 There _____ a lot of water.

4 There _____ much milk in the jar.

5 There _____ a lot of oranges.

6 There _____ a few bananas.

C. Fill in the blanks.

1

There _____ a _____ apples.

2

There _____ _____ apples.

3

There _____ a _____ butter on the bread.

4

There _____ _____ soup in the bowl.

D. Correct the wrong ones.

1 There are much milk in the glass.   is

2 Is there a few milk in the bowl?

3 There is no cucumbers on the plate.

4 Are there no oil in the big bottle?

5 There is a few watermelons at the market.

6 Is there many coins in the jar?

37

Chapter 6 Lesson 3

 Review the grammar points.

Fill in the blanks.

Affirmative	There are **some books** on the shelf.
Question	( ) there ( ) **books** on the shelf?
Answer	Yes, there are ( ) **books**. No, there are ( ) ( ) **books** on the shelf.
Affirmative	There is **some milk** in the bottle.
Question	Is there ( ) **milk** in the bottle?
Answer	Yes, there ( ) ( ) **milk**. No, there is ( ) ( ) **milk** in the bottle.

A. Choose the right ones.

1. Are there   some / any   music books?
   ➡ Yes, there are   some / any   music books.

2. Are there   any / some   new pants in your closet?
   ➡ No, there   is / are   not any new ones.

3. Is there   some / any   pizza on that plate?
   ➡ No, there is not   some / any   pizza on that plate.

4. Do you have   some / any   orange juice?
   ➡ Yes, I have   some / any   orange juice.

5. Does she have any dolls?
   ➡ No, she does not have   any / some   dolls.

6. Are there   some / any   toys in your room?
   ➡ Yes, there are   some / any   toys in my room.

B. Fill in the blanks.

1   A: I am hungry. Do you have _____ bread?

⇒ _____ , I have _____ _____.

2   A: I want some water.

Is there _____ water in the refrigerator?

B: _____ , there is _____ _____ water.

milk

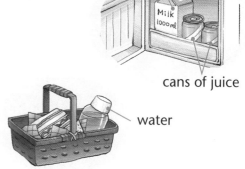

cans of juice

3   A: Does she have any milk?

B: _____ , she _____ _____ any milk.

water

4   A: I need some pencils.

Are there _____ pencils in the drawer?

B: _____ , there _____ _____ pencils in the drawer.

C. Correct the wrong ones.

1   There is ~~any~~ water in the bottle.   some

2   There is some toys on the floor.

3   are there any milk in the refrigerator?

4   There are any cats in our house.

5   There is any money on the table.

6   Is there any books on the shelf?

Memo

First Step in Grammar 2

First Step in Grammar consists of 4 books that enable young learners to learn grammar while they describe things and express ideas related to their daily lives with the learned grammar points. This series aims to motivate young learners to learn grammar through various creative tasks such as problem solving, quizzes, picture descriptions, and various levels of challenging questions. Thus, the content of this book is carefully designed to help young learners integrate information they already know with the learning points in the book by conducting the various task-based activities. This book will be an enjoyable, meaningful guide for young learners as they take their first step in learning English grammar, improving step by step, so that they can achieve their learning goals.

Features

• Facilitates learning the most integral patterns of grammar through image- and task-based activities
• Reinforces key learning with 4-step interactive assessment activities:
  Quick Check, Review Test, Challenge Test, Talking about Pictures and Quiz
• Reinforces the new key learning within the context of cumulative grammar points
• Reflects what most young learners struggle with in mastering grammar
• Provides a two-step Book 1 to help build a successful foundation for early learners

Components

• Student Book 1A, 1B, 2, 3 / Workbook 1A, 1B, 2, 3

Downloadable Resources: www.clueandkey.com
Answer Keys & Other Materials